Why Some Communities Succeed, Why Some Fail—and What to Do About It

Brian Cole

First Printing, 2015

ISBN 978-1507528181

Building Communities, Inc.
155 E. 50th St.
Boise, ID 83714
www.BuildingCommunities.us

Cover design and illustrations: copyright © 2015 by Kevin Bradford.
Contributions provided by Tom Novak.

Dedicated to the other 1%

(See Chapter Three)

FOREWORD

As a small town economic development director, I am constantly challenged by the need to create opportunities, while also ensuring the community protects the things it cherishes. In an effort to maintain the balance, I am constantly seeking out the advice of those who have fought these battles, hoping to absorb useful nuggets of wisdom.

It was through a friend I received a copy of "Why Some Communities Succeed, Why Some Fail—and What To Do About It." In its well-written pages, I found more nuggets than I had hoped for, more than I could readily absorb and the wisdom of someone who has fought more than his share of community and economic development battles.

"Why Some Communities Succeed" is a reference book, a compendium of possibilities and is very much like having a trusted and seasoned advisor at your side. Brian Cole has managed to sort through the maze of an arcane and all-too-often academically frustrating subject without losing his way and without being didactic or condescending.

There is much to be mined, not the least of which is solid advice on the consistently nagging issue of capacity. Conceptual solutions are nice. But these concepts are all they will ever be—good ideas—unless the hurdle of capacity is addressed and overcome up front.

Cole, in assessing the basis of community success, has taken the issue of capacity head on. "For a community to be truly strategic about its future, it must set a course that will ultimately succeed," he writes. "In order to do this, it must select strategies that: 1) build upon comparative advantages, 2) are desired by the people of the community and 3) are supported by the capacity to implement the strategies." Oh how true—financial capacity, political capacity and human capacity.

Small towns are an in-your-face arena where public policy can hinge on personalities and rumors, ignorance and misunderstanding, and an often audible level of distracting and potentially destructive "white noise." But in the end, as Cole points out, success boils down to leadership and to those he calls the "engaged" one percent. Those of us who are given the responsibility of guiding that one percent can only hope and trust that good leaders emerge who will keep them squarely focused on the best interest and future of the community.

We can also be grateful to have someone like Brian Cole around to give us sage advice, keep us well-grounded and reassure us that there is a positive path forward.

> Steve Ayers
> Economic Development Director
> Town of Camp Verde, AZ

Why Some Communities Succeed, Why Some Fail—and What to Do About It

ACKNOWLEDGEMENTS

The theories, tools and practices of community and economic development in this book have been inspired by a professional lifetime of serving communities, regions and states. I therefore dedicate this book to the people who make their communities all they can be.

In particular, I thank John Mitchell, former Chief Economist for U.S. Bank, for his significant scholarly contribution to Chapter Two. In addition, my sincere thanks go to Jennifer Watkins, Kevin Bradford and Karalea Cox for our work "in the trenches" putting the concepts, principles and ideas contained in the book into practice and refining them along the way.

Finally, my greatest respect goes to Dr. Marshall Whitmire who not only helped me to think through every element of the book, but has edited every word from cover to cover.

Why Some Communities Succeed, Why Some Fail—and What to Do About It

TABLE OF CONTENTS

PREFACE   **1**

CHAPTER ONE
The Two-Fruited Tree   **5**

CHAPTER TWO
Largely Uncontrollable National
and International Economic
Megatrends and Forces   **9**

CHAPTER THREE
Civic Condition   **15**

CHAPTER FOUR
Civic Capacity   **31**

CHAPTER FIVE
Civic Strategies and Initiatives   **53**

CHAPTER SIX
Civic Action   **155**

CHAPTER SEVEN
Civic Commitment   **159**

EPILOGUE
Community Success
and the Two-Fruited Tree   **171**

PREFACE

Some pundits claim America's best days are behind us. This book presents a different perspective and provides a path forward—one community at a time—in order to help ensure that America's best days are still ahead.

The economic collapse in the fourth quarter of 2008 followed by a slow—sometimes imperceptible—recovery left many people disillusioned, many communities devastated and an increasing share of the population wondering if and when things would ever get better. However, the recognition that 2015 actually ushered in the 59th consecutive month of job growth is beginning to bolster consumer confidence back to pre-2008 recession levels.

While America may truly be in a significant, sustained recovery, achieving a broad understanding and appreciation of such progress is often frustrated by a national discourse that chronically focuses more on the negative aspects of the economy versus its improvement.

The elevated rancor between political parties at the national level increasingly poisons constructive discourse at the local level. Sadly, Congress, rather than collectively offering solutions, provides the best-known example of this stagnant course of events. One impasse after another undermines our confidence that our nation's largest problems can actually be solved.

This book presents a natural environment metaphor (the Two-Fruited Tree) to explain the work of advancing communities but this preface first uses a human environment paradigm to get our thinking started.

Healthy people have a healthy soul (spiritual health), body (physical health), mind (mental health) and heart (emotional health). We know that people must be proactive to maintain their health in all four of these dimensions of life.

The importance of this book, and what it offers community leaders and volunteers, can be placed in this human context. Our politics and economy over the past six-plus years sets the stage for discussion. After presenting and describing the Two-Fruited Tree in **Chapter One** using a natural environment context, as well as touching on the underlying economic forces that impact our local economies in **Chapter Two**, the next four chapters parallel this soul/body/mind/heart, i.e., human context.

Apathetic and Argumentative <u>Soul</u>[1] (Chapter Three). Congress' repeated inability to work together, to pass and balance a meaningful budget, to authorize payment of accounts payable and to develop a long-term strategic plan for the future of America showcases the combative civic soul of the congressional leaders elected to lead America. When a new U.S. president gets elected and the minority leader of the U.S. Senate states that the primary objective for the next four years is for someone else to get elected U.S. President, you know you live in an Argumentative Stage Country. When the most liberal republican is far to the right of the most conservative democrat, you know you live in an Argumentative Stage Country. When the personal future of Congresspersons is more important to them than the welfare of those who elected them, you know you live in a country that is not functioning well. If American communities are looking to Washington D.C. for a brand of leadership to emulate, American communities are in trouble.

Unfit <u>Body</u> (Chapter Four). Even if America were to replicate and implement the American Recovery and Reinvestment Act (ARRA) of 2009 every year for the next three decades, the nation would still have a crisis in the condition and capacity of its transportation, water and sewer infrastructure! (Few people understand that only $105 billion of the $787 billion was invested in job-creating infrastructure projects. Even less know that the American Society of Civil Engineers estimates that $3.6 *trillion* must be invested by 2020 to ensure needed and safe infrastructure for America.)

The fact is America appears to have an infrastructure disinvestment strategy designed to ensure that the 20th Century was its best. America's current condition and trend for business development capacity is ushering in the Asian Century.

As we recognize that civic capacity includes more than physical infrastructure, it is also alarming to note that cities, counties and states are disinvesting in other forms of capacity such as community and economic development staff, funding for marketing and promotion and funding for research and development.

Myopic <u>Mind</u> (Chapter Five). When communities fail to produce the fruit of community and economic development, they frequently define the problem incorrectly. The executive director gets fired. The budget gets restructured. Board appointments change. But the root of the problem frequently is a community that has selected the wrong strategies and initiatives to begin with (if it has a valid community and economic plan in the first place). Communities that select strategies when they fail to possess the requisite Key Success Factors are doomed to failure.

---

[1] Chapter Three presents the Four Stages of Civic Condition model, which describes the four underlying motivations of community leaders that lead to differing stages of willingness and ability to work together to improve communities.

Elevate this discussion to the United States. What economic strategies and initiatives is our nation advancing? Can you name one? The only apparent strategy is to be in the political majority. The only purpose of being in the majority is to stay there. But to what end? The nation that established industry after industry, built a nationwide transportation system, established the electrical grid and put a man on the moon certainly can devise a coherent and acceptable strategy for the 21st Century.

Weak <u>Heart</u> (Chapter Six). On average, Americans watch 35 hours of television per week. They are now 25 pounds heavier than they were in 1960. Many would rather stay home and complain than show up and help to improve their community.

The sad, if not sick state of our civic discourse, the declining direction of our civic condition and the myopic view of our economic potential would be even more alarming if the nation actually had an army of engaged citizens rolling up their sleeves to do something positive for our future. Unfortunately, with a few exceptions, it doesn't.

Here, Congress is not the poor example. The composition of our Congress is only emulating the people who elected them. Do nothing. Complain about others. Repeat the sequence.

The intrinsic rewards that come from giving time and effort for the betterment of one's town or city are now rarely experienced in many communities. Whether it is the growth of a "me-centered" society, or the increase in alternative forms of entertainment and recreation, the result is that people are increasingly not going to city council or other similar meetings to find out what is going on and to offer their time and talent to improve their community. What was once an expression of heart for others has evolved into a disconnected, what's-in-it-for-me society. America needs a heart transplant.

The Path Forward

This book presents a new paradigm on why some communities succeed, why some fail and what we can do about it. The content is presented in the context of a Two-Fruited Tree—a mythical but relevant and useful concept that draws a parallel between the natural environment and the built environment. On one hand, the science associated with the tree (the natural environment) is well understood and unquestioned (soil, photosynthesis, fruit production, transpiration, etc.). On the other hand, how communities behave and function based on the built environment is far less understood and frequently questioned. This book offers new insights to address this deficiency, specifically related to civic condition, civic capacity, civic strategies/initiatives and civic action.

What Must Change
The only way the *United* States of America can correct its current economic course is to have leaders who are unified and share an *achievement* and/or *actualization* ethic rather than an *apathy* or *argumentative* one. The Two-Fruited Tree is not about winning the next election and controlling the next Congress. The Two-Fruited Tree is about living in the world's most prosperous place and enjoying every minute of it. *Healthy soul.*

The only way the *United* States of America can develop the capacity to move positively forward is to invest in the human, technical, and especially physical infrastructure, necessary to rebuild the country. *Healthy body.*

The only way the *United* States of America will define a positive course is through a serious examination of its own national Key Success Factors, and then to develop policy and strategies consistent with such comparative advantages. *Healthy mind.*

The only way that the *United* States of America will make the 21st Century its best century is for its people to decide in their heart that this nation is worth fighting for, and now is the time to act one community at a time. *Healthy heart.*

It may be too much to expect our Congress can and will move beyond the argumentative body politic that destroys its possibility of leading this much-needed change. It is not too late, however, for local community leaders who generally do not wear their party label on their lapel to lead this nation one community at a time. For such community leaders to do this, they will have to master the soul, body, mind and heart of their cities and counties. It can be done.

Despite the poor example at the national level, there are communities at the Action Stage, and even the Alliance Stage, throughout the nation. The leaders of these successful communities know they must subordinate their personal interests to the community interests. These communities exist. They are our best hope as they serve as powerful models for the change that is needed.

CHAPTER ONE
The Two-Fruited Tree

CHAPTER ONE
The Two-Fruited Tree

Every day we get bombarded by economic statistics. Gross Domestic Product. Aggregate demand. Consumer spending. Government spending. Housing prices. Exports. Imports. Interest rates. Consumer confidence. Tax rates. Economic stimulus. Currency value. Labor productivity. Factory inventories. Unemployment rates. Technological innovation. Commodity prices. And on and on.

What do these factors and their associated megatrends and forces all have in common? They are largely uncontrollable by the very people who are on the front lines working to improve the economy.

While at first one might think that the economic development front lines are staffed primarily by the federal elected leaders of the country, the truth is that there are many times more local leaders and volunteers working to make the nation a better place. In the United States, there are 535 people in Congress. There are well over 18,000 cities and towns. It is the people at the local level who care the most about their community, and they are on the front lines for America's future.

This book is about these local people and their quest for better economic conditions and improved quality of life in cities and towns across the nation. While the macroeconomic factors of the nation and world inevitably have an impact on local economies, the forces associated with them are below the surface and largely unreachable by city managers, county managers, economic development directors and other local professionals dedicated to community and economic development.

The figure at right, the *Two-Fruited Tree*, not only presents these sub-surface (uncontrollable) economic factors, but it presents a full spectrum of forces that shape the future of American (and worldwide) communities. This bio-mimicry shows the uncontrollable (subsurface) and controllable (above the surface) factors impacting communities, as well as the relationship among such factors.

Below the soil surface are the uncontrollable national and international economic forces that, while they do impact local economic conditions, are well beyond the grasp of local decision makers.

On the surface is the civic condition of the local community. This surface soil layer is so thin that it is rarely detected by the very people it impacts, and yet serves to predict the future success (or lack thereof) of community and economic development activities.

Then there is the tree. The two trunks represent: 1) the business and economic development capacity (jobs), and 2) the community and quality-of-life capacity (livability) of the community. The relative strength of the trunks is the foundation for producing the fruit (planned outcomes of community and economic development activities).

The fruit on the tree, depicted by the two shapes (pears and apples), represents: 1) the business development (job creating) strategies, and 2) the community development (quality-of-life-producing) strategies.

Finally, the leaves represent the energy of the community taking the actions needed to produce and harvest the fruit (jobs and quality of life).

The future of our communities, therefore, is shaped by:

- **Largely Uncontrollable National and International Economic Megatrends and Forces (CHAPTER TWO)**
- **Civic Condition (CHAPTER THREE)**
- **Civic Capacity (CHAPTER FOUR)**
- **Civic Strategies and Initiatives (CHAPTER FIVE)**
- **Civic Action (CHAPTER SIX)**
- **Civic Commitment (CHAPTER SEVEN)**

The success of communities to envision and enact their future is therefore determined by *actions* that implement *strategies* supported by *capacity* all undergirded by *civic condition*. While the uncontrollable factors are always present, they are largely trivial to communities focused on defining and implementing their desired future.

Ultimately, there are two goals for communities: sound, diversified economies and high quality of life. The field of community and economic development is dedicated to pursuing these goals. This book presents a new paradigm for understanding, planning and implementing the strategies and initiatives to achieve these goals.

Recognizing the Uncontrollable Forces

Chapter Two introduces and describes some of the major national and international economic megatrends and forces that impact communities. While it is beneficial to begin with an exploration and understanding of these factors, it is important for communities to recognize that they should not waste their energy trying to change them.

CHAPTER TWO
Largely Uncontrollable National and International Economic Megatrends and Forces

CHAPTER TWO
Largely Uncontrollable National and International Economic Megatrends and Forces

Community and economic development is all about positively influencing the direction of towns, cities, counties, tribes and other communities. Influence is based upon the ability to impact and change events and circumstances. However, this chapter is primarily about things on which community advocates have little or no control: national and international economic megatrends and forces. Nevertheless, it is wise to have some idea about the trends and patterns in the wider economy that may present opportunities and challenges for local communities—the big things that shape the environment in which community advocates function.

These trends and forces definitely impact local economic conditions. The price of agricultural commodities affects many rural communities that depend upon the harvesting and processing of such products. The value of currency impacts local economies that depend upon international tourism for their well-being. The general state of the economy impacts the ability of communities to recruit expanding companies.

In short, the condition of the national and international economy is a major factor impacting, among other things, the local unemployment rate, local housing prices and local income levels.

> "A region's economy floats on a national (perhaps global) sea,
> while being buffeted by local tides and winds."
>
> (McNees and Tootell, July, 1991 *New England Economic Review*)

Throughout this book, a parallel is drawn between local community and economic development, and the mythical Two-Fruited Tree. Here we begin with what holds up the tree—the earth. Specifically, deep beneath the surface of our communities is the earth's bedrock—a solid layer that lies beneath the loose surface deposits of soil. Unreachable. Impenetrable. Yet, it is a solid foundation.

Similarly, national and international megatrends and forces are fundamentally beyond the influence of local community leaders. While such large-scale economic dynamics either lift or depress local economic conditions, they are "miles" below the surface.

From time to time, the earth shakes (in 1929 and 2008, e.g.), the economy collapses and communities fall. At other times the national and international economy forms a solid foundation for local economic growth.

The media provides us with daily doses of information, including measures and estimates of national performance. Non-stop talking heads opine on the importance of minor changes in soon-to-be-revised numbers.

Where to Focus
So what should we pay some attention to?

Quarterly, we have estimates of Real Gross Domestic Product (GDP) which is the total value of the output of goods and services in the United States. Every first Friday of the month brings the employment/unemployment estimates, and every Thursday initial unemployment claims are released. The list goes on and on, and many of the numbers are subsequently revised—a fact often overlooked.

Local and regional data are available less frequently, and often with long lag times. The Bureau of Economic Analysis website has county and metro area data such as personal income and output.

Macroeconomic policy is formulated by Congress and the President in the case of fiscal policy (federal taxing and spending), and by the Federal Reserve in the case of monetary policy. What happens with policy development and change, about which there is much disagreement, posturing and political conflict, is simply background information for local decision makers.

Current Conditions
At the start of 2015, after five years of near two-percent growth, the nation appeared poised for acceleration amid a world economy whose performance had deteriorated. Employment had surpassed its previous peak, net worth had recovered and the fiscal drag had diminished after the 2013 fiscal cliff. Oil prices collapsed due to increased supply and moderating demand, boosting real income for consumers. The Federal Reserve completed its tapering in October of 2014 when the bond purchase program ended and is proceeding to the next phase of unwinding its extraordinary efforts to support the economy.

These are dynamics to be aware of--something that can be accomplished by reading the nation's business press—The Wall Street Journal, Business Week and The Economist, for example. Community leaders, for example can read the one-page statement that is released after the meetings of the Federal Reserve Open Market Committee and the Beige Book which comes out from the Fed two weeks prior to the meetings, which reviews conditions across the nation. Many states have state-specific forecasts as a part of the revenue estimation and budget process that are available on-line.

In the second decade of the 21st Century, local decision making is taking place in the aftermath of the most serious downturn in most people's memories. Home prices plummeted, net worth declined and millions of jobs were lost. The rebound has been slow, but persistent. Employment gains are widespread across the nation. Incomes have lagged but tighter labor markets should help. The nature of the recent experience has rekindled interest in growth and development and efforts to increase incomes.

The looming new world will be an older one demographically. The population is aging, the workforce is growing more slowly and the proportion of retirees is expanding. Older consumers have different spending patterns, which can bring opportunity, as well as challenges.

Finding people with desired skill sets may be more of a problem in a time of slower labor force growth. The Bureau of Labor Statistics projects annual labor force growth of 0.7 percent between 2010 and 2020, little more than half the 1.3 percent growth rate between 1990 and 2000. The number of 16-24 year-olds is expected to decline by 1.3 percent per year, while those over 55 will increase by 3.3 percent per year.

The above is the kind of background information about the larger economic environment in which local community leaders will function. The Two-Fruited Tree must take root in a world where many factors are determined and influenced elsewhere. Some awareness is needed but actions should focus on the things that can be directly influenced.

The Somewhat Controllable Uncontrollable
There is one major exception to this "Avoid the Uncontrollables" rule that relates to a basic assumption made throughout this book, i.e., community and economic development activity is conducted in locations where there is a stable foundation of reasonably effective governance.

For example, one of the most important considerations made by international businesses is the presence of stable national governments, including a body of fair and functioning contract and regulatory laws. Without a responsive, predictable governmental system, community development—and especially business and economic development—activities will be very difficult to carry out, if they can be carried out at all.

One does not have to go beyond the borders of the United States to find such dysfunctional governmental systems. Many Native American Indian Tribes, for example, struggle to create and manage governmental structures that effectively advance their economy and quality of life.

Further, for community and economic development activities to be successful, government must be an effective and active partner with legitimate business and non-profit entities. At the community level, community and economic development activities must be envisioned, discussed, planned, budgeted, managed and evaluated. While business and non-profit organizations play a vital role in these efforts, there is no substitute for effective local government involvement in these activities.

At higher levels of government (state and federal—and tribal), the provision of community and economic development programs and incentives are vital to inspire and facilitate desired progress.

Using the two-fruited-tree metaphor, the involvement of government in community and economic activities might be "below the surface," but it is not so low as to be totally uncontrollable (per the figure, think of these as the "moveable boulders" below the surface, yet above the bedrock).

In fact, proactive efforts to improve governance structures and participation in these activities are absolutely imperative. Such efforts, however, should not be conducted separately from other community and economic development activities. It requires simultaneously working to advance a community and making critical improvements in the governance process in order to create the necessary incentive for such improvements to occur. That is, without pursuing the fruit—job creation and quality-of-life enhancements—at the same time, the arduous task of modifying government processes and possibly structure will typically fizzle out. Likewise, the absence of government reform will ultimately complicate and frustrate community and economic development activities, and consequently reduce, if not entirely prevent, achieving beneficial results.

The focus on efficient and effective government processes and structure is, in effect, the bridge between a discussion of "uncontrollable factors" and civic condition/civic capacity.

Ineffective governance substantially diminishes civic capacity, and typically renders civic condition to an Apathy or Argumentative Stage. For a fuller description of these dynamics, see Chapters Three and Four.

From Uncontrollable Forces to Civic Condition

Next, Chapter Three will shift us from the world of uncontrollable factors to the very thin connection point between uncontrollables and controllables: civic condition.

Just as the thin layer of soil on the Two-Fruited Tree graphic is nearly indistinguishable, civic condition goes nearly unnoticed by the people advancing their community. Nearly unnoticed...but highly influential to the community's ultimate ability to envision and enact its future.

Why Some Communities Succeed, Why Some Fail—and What to Do About It

CHAPTER THREE
Civic Condition

CHAPTER THREE
Civic Condition

The *civic condition* of a community is the soil surface that lies between the uncontrollable sub-surface economic factors and the above-surface Two-Fruited Tree. This critical element is explained by the ***Four Stages of Civic Condition*** model, which provides insight into the underlying dynamics that are the foundation for successful (or unsuccessful) community and economic development planning and implementation.

This surface layer is, in effect, the soil from which our Two-Fruited Tree draws its nutrients. If the soil is inert and/or rocky, the tree will not produce fruit. If the soil has the right texture, structure, chemical and biological characteristics, our tree can grow and prosper.

Just as soil conditions are the foundation for a healthy and productive tree, the intent and quality of a community's civic discourse and interaction drives the potential future success (or lack thereof) of community and economic development efforts.

If you were to split the earth into two halves at the equator and examine it, the surface layer at the outside edge would be so thin as to be virtually undetectable. At the same time, the surface of the earth covers the entire planet. The surface is under every city, every county and every nation. It is this thin, almost undetectable layer that perhaps best serves to answer the question: "Why do some communities succeed and some communities fail?"

This will be become quite evident, if not profound, in the next three chapters as we explore and focus on what is most detectable and relatively much more controllable by communities: civic capacity, civic strategies and initiatives, and civic action.

Civic capacity—the human, financial and technical resources of a community—can be budgeted, increased, decreased, focused and directed.

Civic strategies and initiatives—the specific direction a community chooses—can be selected, timed, emphasized and deemphasized.

Civic action—the specific activities a community implements to advance strategies and initiatives—can be enacted, delegated, ordered and tabled.

Civic condition just *is*. Although Chapter Seven offers recommendations on how to influence, or at least work with civic condition, the fact is influencing civic condition is nearly as difficult as detecting it in the first place.

Better understanding the characteristics and effects of civic condition is the secret ingredient that largely explains why communities with similar civic capacities, similar

Key Success Factors, similar strategies, similar initiatives and similar action steps can experience such differing outcomes.

Why is it that one community advances projects like clockwork and other communities seem to stand still? Just look at the thin, almost undetectable layer of civic discourse and interaction: civic condition.

THE FOUR STAGES OF CIVIC CONDITION

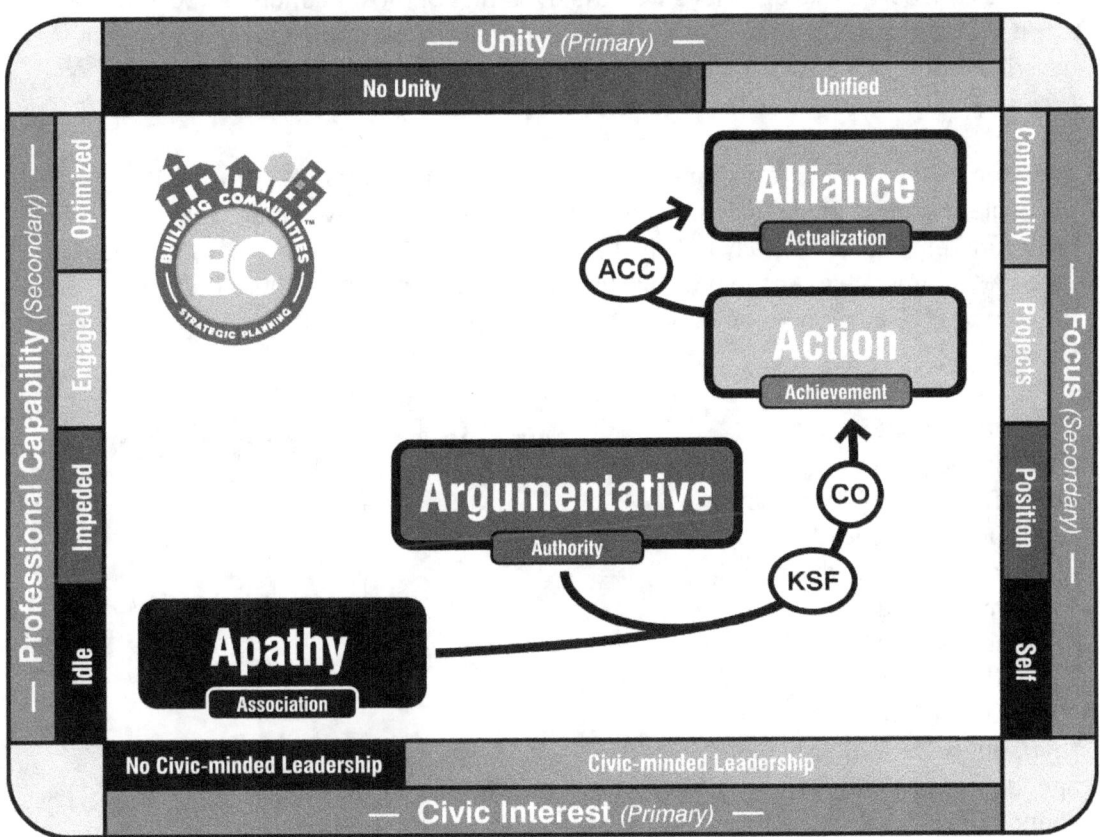

ACC = Alliance Community Commitment | CO = Community Organizer Assessment | KSF = Key Success Factor Analysis

Framework of the Model

The model ultimately places communities at one of four *stages* of civic condition based upon four factors. Two of the factors are *primary* (Civic Interest and Unity), and two are *secondary* (Focus and Professional Capability).

The primary factors explain which stage the community is in, while the secondary ones explain the dynamics within the community at each stage. The Focus secondary factor also serves to place communities at the highest stage of condition in the very rare circumstances in which the upmost levels of capacity are achieved and the community truly desires to actualize its ultimate potential.

Primary Factors (Civic Interest and Unity). The primary factors are the most powerful predictors of the civic condition of a community.

Before explaining more about these two factors, it is important to understand the context in which communities envision and enact their future.

It has been said the "world is run by those who show up." This certainly seems true when it comes to advancing community and economic development initiatives. Whereas the 80/20 rule describes well the dynamics of most economics (80% of the effects come from 20% of the causes—the Pareto Principle), the 99/1 rule generally describes community and economic development (1% of the population commits its time and effort for the sole purpose of benefiting their community).

Therefore, these Civic Interest and Unity factors pertain to this 1%. While it is certainly desirable to expect more than just 1% to participate in local civic endeavors, unfortunately this is generally not the case. NOTE: Much has been discussed about "the 1%" in America over the past five years. "The 1%" described here is different—not based upon the accumulation of wealth, but rather based upon the contribution to society.

Civic Interest. *Civic Interest* explains the primary orientation—motivation—of community leaders. Do they have an interest in advancing the community as a whole? Are they focused on the welfare of the entire community, not just their personal interests? Do they subordinate their personal agenda to the community agenda?

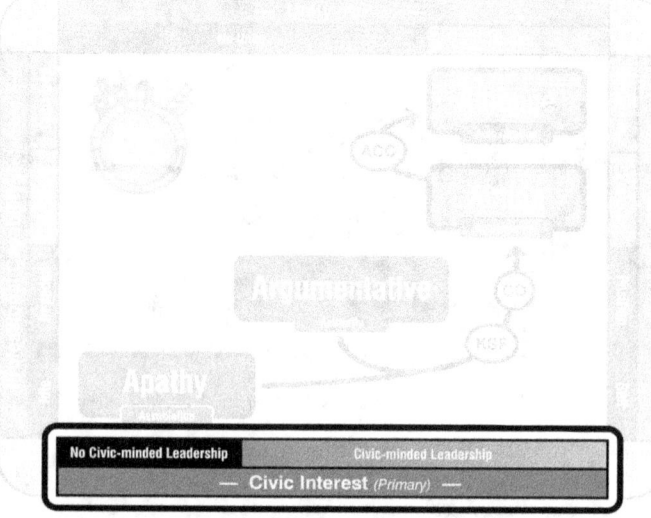

THE FOUR STAGES OF CIVIC CONDITION

Without strong civic-minded leadership, there is little or no drive to advance a collective community agenda. In such circumstances, communities may be comprised of wonderful people with laudable values related to family, education, health and assisting the disadvantaged but they fail to see such pursuits in a broader community context.

The result for communities without a broader Civic Interest is the Stage of Apathy. **Apathy Communities** are characterized by a peaceful civic setting, modest community pursuits and a general acceptance of the status quo.

Civic Interest forms the foundation of the model, and is depicted on the bottom X-axis. Communities without civic-minded leadership are by default Apathy Communities. Only when communities benefit from civic-minded leadership can they ascend from this stage.

Unity. The second primary factor is *Unity*. In our model, Unity is a broad common agreement about the strategic direction of a community.

Unity is irrelevant in Apathy Communities. There is no need to have agreement about community direction in a community that has no civic interest (or collective direction) to begin with.

Communities with Civic Interest without Unity are **Argumentative Communities**. These are communities that have a collective desire for better times, and yet have no common acceptance of a path to realize such conditions. Such communities are characterized by advocacy groups (or individuals) that have a vision and plan for the future, only to find opposing interests working to impede or stop their efforts and goals.

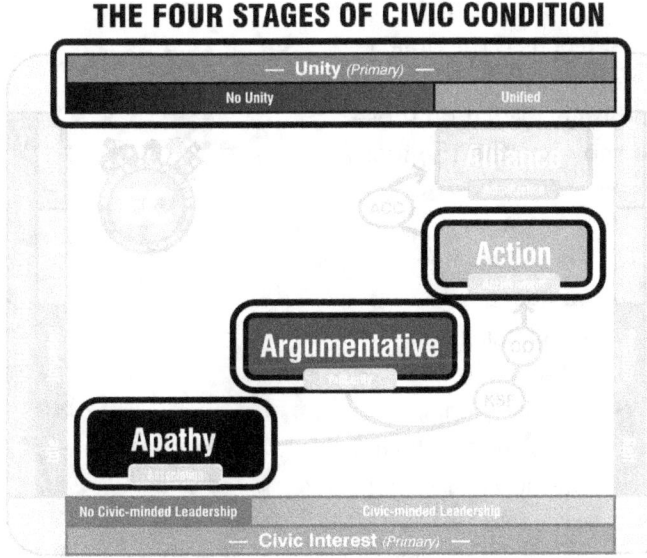

THE FOUR STAGES OF CIVIC CONDITION

Unity is the separator between Argumentative Communities and higher-stage communities. While the lack of Unity relegates the community to the status of the Argumentative stage, communities that achieve a common agreement about their future have significant opportunities for community advancement.

Communities with both Civic Interest and Unity are **Action Communities.** Such communities are characterized by a never-ending series of achievements in community and business development. Projects are advanced like clockwork. The ribbon-cutting ceremony is barely completed before the next groundbreaking ceremony is being planned.

Unity forms the top of the model, and is depicted on the top X-axis. It is only with Unity that the top two stages of civic condition can be reached.

Secondary Factors (Focus and Professional Capability). Before introducing the highest stage of condition, it is important to introduce the two secondary factors: *Focus* and *Professional Capability*.

Focus. Focus is the object of the game within any community. What do those who show up (the 1%) focus on?

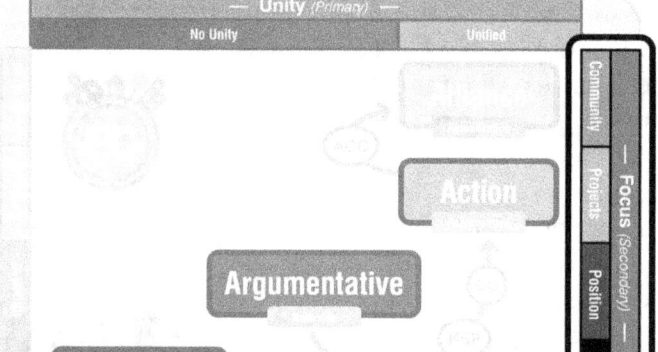

- For communities without an overarching Civic Interest, there remains nothing to focus on other than the individual desires of people. For these Apathy Communities, the focus therefore is on *self*.

- For communities with an overarching Civic Interest but lacking Unity, the focus becomes maintaining or advancing the individual *positions* of the community actors. People advocate their positions in order to gain ground in what they perceive is a give-and-take, win-lose world, which ultimately becomes lose-lose and chaotic. Example: the current U.S. Congress.

- For communities with both Civic Interest and Unity, the focus is on the advancement of one or more *projects*. The advancement of the community is virtually universally accepted, and the method for advancement is investing in the future of the community for business and community development purposes.

Considering the Focus of the community leaders introduces the fourth stage of civic condition.

Why Some Communities Succeed, Why Some Fail—and What to Do About It

- Communities that elevate their focus from projects to the *community* itself become **Alliance Communities.** This stage is very rare, as such communities not only have Civic Interest and Unity, but they clearly focus on the overall interests of the community— frequently by subordinating the advancement of one project to another.

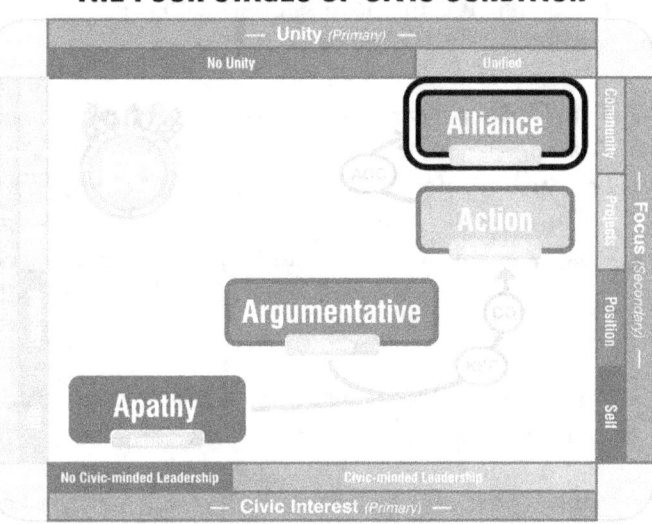

Each civic stage, therefore, has its specific Focus: Apathy Communities focus on self, Argumentative Communities focus on positions, Action Communities focus on projects and Alliance Communities focus on the overall advancement of the community itself.

Professional Capability.

Unlike the other three factors (Civic Interest, Unity and Focus), which relate to the "1%" (the people who "show up"), the fourth factor relates to the people paid to conduct the "business of community advancement." These people are the city managers, public works directors, chamber of commerce directors, visitor and convention bureau managers, economic development directors, port managers, downtown development directors and others in key positions of public trust.

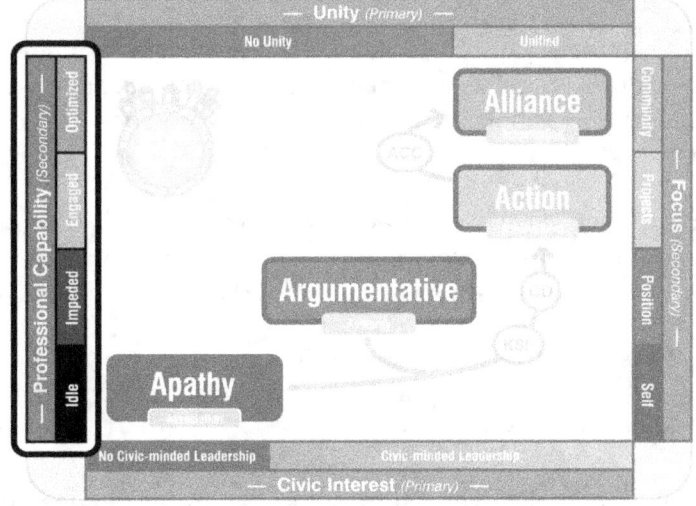

If Unity represents the steering wheel of the community, then Professional Capability is the gas pedal. It is the professionals who primarily carry out the activities necessary to bring the projects and initiatives to fruition.

While professional capability is essential for community advancement, the civic condition has a greater effect on the Professional Capability than vice versa. That is, the application of Professional Capability is either impeded, or enabled, by civic condition.

- Apathy Communities, characterized by an acceptance of the status quo, generally keep their professionals *idle* as there is little to do beyond the basic operations of paying the bills and "keeping the lights on."

- Argumentative Communities, characterized by a constant churning of tensions and battles, *impede* the work of local professionals.

- Action Communities, characterized by systematically advancing projects, keep professionals *engaged* in the day-to-day work of improving the community.

- Alliance Communities, characterized by becoming all the community can be, make *optimal use* of the time and talents of local professionals.

Community Motivation Theory

The *Four Stages of Civic Condition* model is complemented by the *Community Motivation Theory*. This theory postulates that a very small percentage of any community's population defines and dominates its civic stage.

In a community of 10,000 people, therefore, approximately 100 (i.e., 1%) *activist* individuals typically volunteer to serve in elected, appointed or other community service leadership positions. An even smaller percentage—10% of the 1% (0.1%)—are *super-activists*.

It is the collective motivation of this "group of 0.1%" that sets the civic tone of the community. There are four distinct underlying motivations that characterize the super-activists: 1) association, 2) authority, 3) achievement and 4) actualization.

It is the collective motivation of the super-activists that helps enable or impede the civic agenda of a community, and sets the stage for the strategic planning—and plan implementation—process.

There is typically a very strong interrelationship between the motivation of the super-activists and the civic stage of the community:

- Apathy Stage Communities tend to be driven by *association*-oriented super-activists. These people interrelate civically simply for the experience of socializing.

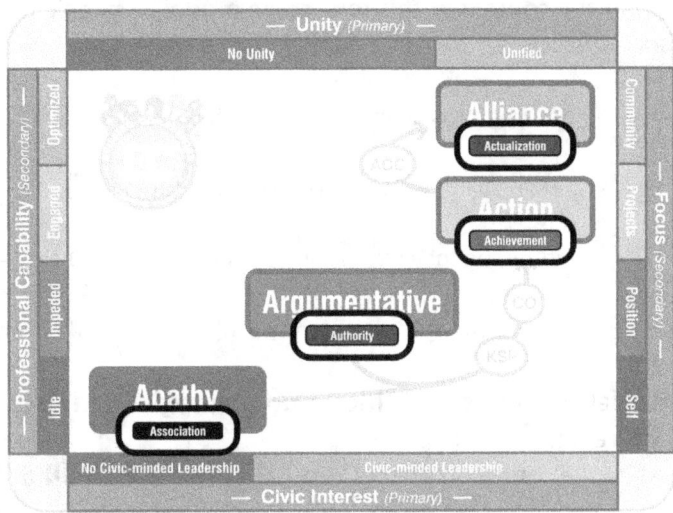

THE FOUR STAGES OF CIVIC CONDITION

- Argumentative Stage Communities are dominated by super-activists who strive to maintain and enhance their *authority*. While the civics of the community may have the flavor of teamwork and cooperation, the underlying dynamic is control.

- Action Stage Communities are characterized by super-activists with a drive for *achievement*. This motivation matches that of the broader 1% volunteer base.

- Alliance Stage Communities are led by super-activists who desire the holistic advancement of the entire community, and are primarily motivated to *actualize* the community's ultimate potential.

Understanding the prevailing civic motivation can be very helpful, if not crucial, to participants in a community strategic planning process.

Because participants in the process (the 1%) are typically driven by *achievement*, it is frequently difficult for them to understand the motivations of the super-activists, if their prevailing motivation is *association* or *authority* (vs. *achievement* or *actualization*). Heightened awareness of this dynamic can help community volunteers become more effective—or at least more understanding of the challenges that lie ahead. (See the "Considering Civic Condition" sub-section of Chapter Seven for more about how participants in community development planning and implementation can effectively navigate their civic condition stage.)

The Role of Strategic Planning

Within the context of this four-stage model, strategic planning has several important functions:

- Encouraging civic-minded leadership

- Creating a unified view toward the future

- Shifting the focus from self and positions to projects and community

- Creating engaged community professionals and optimizing their performance

Interface of Civic Condition and Strategic Planning

Local reaction to the planning and implementation phases of a community and economic development strategic planning process is distinct and somewhat predictable depending on the community's civic condition stage.

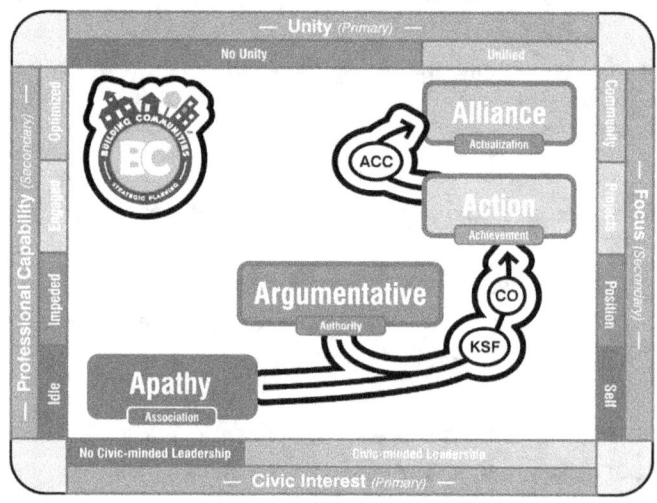

THE FOUR STAGES OF CIVIC CONDITION

ACC = Alliance Community Commitment | CO = Community Organizer Assessment | KSF = Key Success Factor Analysis

Apathy Stage. Communities in the Apathy Stage provide a fascinating study of the planning process. During the planning phase, people show up, show interest, participate and appear set for progress. Unfortunately, that is very often where progress stops.

When the community shifts to the implementation phase, nothing happens. The proverbial "report sitting on the shelf" is all too often the result.

Argumentative Stage. Planning and implementation in the Argumentative Stage is very challenging. Typically, a small group of behind-the-scenes individuals desire to

Reactions to the Planning and Implementation Process		
Civic Condition	Planning Phase	Implementation Phase
Apathy	Enjoyable, Positive	Disengaged, Disinterested
Argumentative	Regimented, Controlled	Selective, Forced
Action	Engaging, Productive	Collaborative, Effective
Alliance	Studious, Complete	Deliberate, Purposeful

control most, if not all, aspects of the planning effort in order that their agenda becomes codified through a process that appears to be a collective community endeavor.

Action Stage. Strategic planning in an Action Stage community is a positive experience for virtually everyone involved. The planning phase reinforces existing efforts, inspires new initiatives and galvanizes teamwork. Action-oriented people desire and work toward the completion of an objective and comprehensive roadmap for their future.

Alliance Stage. It is very rare that a community evolves to the Alliance Stage. A paradigm shift from project-focus to community-focus characterizes this phase. It requires strong and sustained local leadership to achieve this condition. A planning process for a community in the Alliance Stage can be very successful, providing it does not become all-encompassing—planning only for the sake of planning.

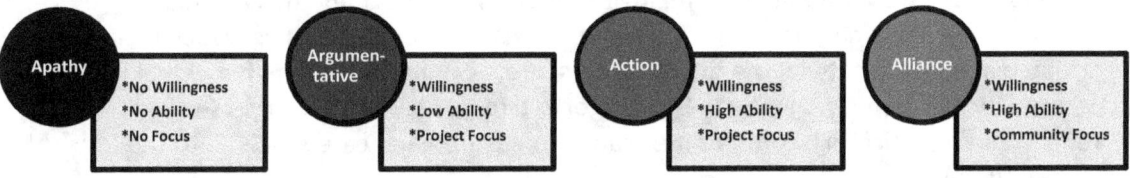

At the civic stage level, strategic planning is about transforming Apathy and Argumentative Communities into Action (and ultimately Alliance) Communities.

This transformation is best done through a very comprehensive, objective, expeditious and action-oriented strategic planning process (Chapter Seven) that enables communities to establish the capacity to implement their priorities (Chapter Four), select strategies and initiatives that have the highest likelihood of success (Chapter Five) and then self-define a series of action steps designed to initiate implementation activity (Chapter Six). In effect, mobilizing the community through implementing a well-crafted, community-supported community and economic development strategic plan is the best way to elevate civic condition from Apathy and Argumentative behavior. Such activity reinforces the achievement motivation, while giving purpose to the association motivation (Apathy Stage) and working to overcome the authority motivation (Argumentative Stage).[2]

---

[2] *Note that the author of this book has established a community and economic development strategic planning company, Building Communities (www.BuildingCommunities.us), that offers a very specific process consistent with the principles and objectives outlined in this book. Three specific tools have been designed to facilitate the planning process: the Key Success Factor Analysis, the Community Organizer Assessment and the Alliance Community Commitment. These tools are built into a 14-hour (seven-session) process called Plan Week that efficiently enables local Steering Committee members and the general public to develop their plan.*

Isolation is a friend to communities in the Apathy and Argumentative Stages. Without bringing the community together to collectively envision and enact its future, the very simple association motivation, as well as the corrosive authority motivation persist— and the people who have most at stake in the future of their communities are rendered ineffective.

Sometimes the movies capture it best. Here is a quote from President Shepherd, portrayed by Michael Douglas in <u>The American President</u>: *"America isn't easy. America is advanced citizenship. You gotta want it bad, 'cause it's gonna put up a fight."*

Measuring Civic Condition

Unlike the objective nature of evaluating and improving capacity, considering and selecting strategies, and even assigning specific implementation action steps, addressing civic condition is very subjective. It is one thing to generally agree on what civic condition stage a community may be in, it is another to determine this through more rigorous, objective analysis. This can be accomplished, however, using a social science research approach that yields a quantitative score. Similar to how an individual's personality and temperament can be categorized (e.g., by using the Myers-Briggs Temperament Indicator), communities can be measured and categorized into the four civic conditions.

The *Civic Condition Assessment* is an instrument designed to help community leaders and volunteers conduct a more systematic examination of their civic stage. They can receive a high-level understanding of the prevailing civic motivation of their community by using the following tool, which asks respondents to select the best of the four descriptions for each of the following scenarios.

1. Local public hearings are conducted primarily to:
   a) Have an open discussion about an issue or project

   b) Meet the legal requirements for decision making

   c) Set the basis for addressing an issue or advancing a project

   d) Consider how a topic relates to the community

2. The top leaders of the community can best be described as:
   a) Friendly

   b) Powerful

   c) Effective

   d) Thoughtful

3. Professional community staff in key development positions (city managers, development personnel, port executives, etc.) are hired and employed by their governing bodies because they are:
   a) Affable, pleasant

   b) Submissive, loyal

   c) Effective, connected

   d) Intelligent, studious

4. The general public describes its community's leadership as:
   a) Part of the family

   b) Good ol' boys

   c) Professional leaders

   d) Intellectuals

5. Major community decisions and deals are made:
   a) Rarely

   b) In smoke-filled rooms

   c) In open public forums

   d) Regularly based on established procedures

6. Community members who go to state-level conferences primarily participate by:
   a) Attending

   b) Determining the conference topics and speakers

   c) Presenting new ideas and receiving awards

   d) Contributing to the conversation at the event

7. Projects in the community are:
   a) Rarely advanced

   b) Debated

   c) Completed

   d) Advanced with the long-term in mind

8. Budget shortfalls in the community are addressed by:
   a) Lamenting the loss of programs and services and/or staff positions

   b) Axing programs and services and/or staff positions not supported by the community's formal leaders

   c) Creative funding and/or partnerships

   d) Formulating viable long-term solutions

9. Newspaper editorials primarily focus on:
   a) Honoring people and milestones

   b) Failures and foibles

   c) Effort and achievement

   d) Purpose and procedures

10. In general, civic and business leaders view their elected officials as:
    a) Irrelevant

    b) Obstacles

    c) Partners

    d) Philosophers

11. If the Governor comes to town, the agenda is:
    a) The Governor's

    b) Controlled, closed

    c) The community's

    d) Consistent with state priorities

12. The most popular sections in the local newspaper are:
    a) Sports, living, obituaries

    b) Public notices, police blotter

    c) Metro, regional, local

    d) Front page, editorial

13. Priority community projects primarily relate to:
    a) Public celebrations of culture and history

    b) Erecting monuments and statues

    c) Civic improvements

    d) Establishment and operation of Institutes

14. The Donors' Wall at the local civic facility is:
    a) Dotted with the names of many small contributors

    b) Headed by recognizing key officials

    c) Lengthy with contributions grouped by funding categories

    d) Precise with the names, titles and contribution of the donors

15. Arriving five minutes early to a city council meeting, you are most apt to note:
    a) Refreshments

    b) Councilors and staff talking amongst themselves

    c) Councilors and staff mingling with the general public

    d) Posted community vision and/or mission statement

16. The entrance sign(s) welcoming you to the community is:
    a) Adorned with fresh flowers

    b) Stately and structured

    c) Accompanied by signs of civic organizations

    d) Proclaiming the local mission statement or slogan

17. Over the past 20 years, our mayors have primarily been:
    a) A friend to all

    b) The ruler

    c) The doer

    d) The parliamentarian

18. If the high school sports team were to win the state championship, the city council would:
    a) Throw a party

    b) Acknowledge the achievement under Other Business

    c) Discuss their first-hand experience with the team at a council meeting

    d) Invite the team to a council meeting and recognize them

19. When a community hero or benefactor dies, the community:
    a) Holds a potluck

    b) Has a small ceremony is his/her honor

    c) Has a ceremony that focuses on his/her contributions

    d) Builds a memorial in his/her honor

20. When a new company announces it is coming to town, the community:
    a) Cannot remember when this last happened

    b) Listens to the mayor's speech and watches the ribbon being cut

    c) Considers what other businesses can be attracted to town

    d) Considers how the business and community can work together

If you wish to take the Civic Condition Assessment and score your perception of the Civic Condition Stage of your community, visit http://www.buildingcommunities.us/civic-condition-assessment.html.

From Civic Condition to Civic Capacity

Next, Chapter Four moves us full circle from the uncontrollable megatrends and forces, and the somewhat controllable civic condition to the very controllable civic capacity.

As shown by the Two-Fruited Tree, civic capacity is what supports the ultimate objectives of the community (a strong economy and improved quality of life).

CHAPTER FOUR
Civic Capacity

CHAPTER FOUR
Civic Capacity

Next we consider what is above the surface of community and economic development work—civic capacity. While communities must be wary of becoming preoccupied with what is below the surface (uncontrollable factors) and must be mindful of what is on the surface (civic condition), they must also take a comprehensive and objective look at their *capacity* to conduct the work. This is represented by the double trunk of the Two-Fruited Tree.

The double trunk represents two distinct forms of capacity: Business development (job-creating capacity), which requires one set of elements and community development (quality-of-life-producing capacity), which requires another set.

Before introducing the specific elements of capacity, it is worthwhile to examine the relationship between civic condition and community and business development capacity. Just as a tree will not produce fruit without the ability to draw nutrients from healthy soil, a community cannot advance itself without healthy civic discourse and interaction. Regardless of capacity, a community that is generally indifferent (Apathy Stage) or embattled (Argumentative Stage) rarely effectively engages its human, financial and technical resources to implement strategies. The best community staff, most robust community budgets and most sophisticated technical resources rarely get deployed well (if at all) when either of the two lowest levels of civic condition prevail.

Conversely, communities in the Action Stage or Alliance Stage are poised to make the most out of their community and business development capacity. Human, financial and technical resources, even if meager, can be very effectively utilized to implement multiple community and economic development strategies.

Healthy civic condition coupled with strong capacity is a recipe for tremendous community progress—progress that produces future success. Maintaining such condition and capacity over time creates communities that are renowned for their quality of life and economic opportunities.

Defining Capacity. Capacity, as it relates to community and economic development, is the human, financial and technical ability of a community to implement strategies.

Human capacity relates to the people who are paid or volunteer to help implement community priorities. In addition to volunteers who contribute their time and talent, paid professionals include city managers, county managers, port managers, chamber executives, economic development directors, convention and visitor bureau directors, downtown managers, regional council executives and many others.

Financial capacity relates to the monetary resources available to the community to invest in staffing, training, promotion, planning, infrastructure and other purposes.

Technical capacity relates to the expertise on which the community can draw from its public and private sector, as well as from people outside the community who have a stake in its future. People who lend their technical capacity to communities are extension agents, economists, energy company executives, bankers, consultants, business counselors, communications experts, social media professionals, human resources professionals and others.

The specific talents and expertise needed to implement business development (job creating and retaining) strategies is largely distinct from expertise needed to implement community development (quality-of-life producing) strategies. While there is some overlap, the presentation of capacity for these two community priorities is separated here. Business development capacity is presented first, followed by community development capacity.

Similar to measuring civic condition through the Civic Condition Assessment, capacity can be measured by the Community Organizer Assessment. More on how to score your community utilizing this assessment can be found at www.buildingcommunities.us/community-organizer-assessment.html.

BUSINESS DEVELOPMENT CAPACITY

While there are dozens of factors that contribute to the capacity of a community to both define and implement business development strategies, these factors can be grouped into seven distinct Business Development Capacity elements:

- Business Development Strategy

- Local Staff and Team Development

- Industrial Land and Infrastructure

- Targeted Industries

- Marketing

- Prospect and Lead Management

- Closing the Deal

Element One: Business Development Strategy. The community needs to determine its desire for—and commitment to—business development, and then outline specific approaches to achieve results.

Element Two: Local Staff and Team Development. It takes the combination of professional staff and community volunteers to proactively pursue business development activities.

Element Three: Industrial Land and Infrastructure. Available, cost-competitive land and infrastructure are essential ingredients for existing and prospective businesses.

Element Four: Targeted Industries. Focusing the business development objectives is required in order to effectively attract new businesses.

Element Five: Marketing. A variety of marketing approaches, ranging from simple and inexpensive to complex and costly, can be employed to reach prospects.

Element Six: Prospect and Lead Management. Quickly and professionally responding to business development prospects is fundamental to creating jobs.

Element Seven: Closing the Deal. Landing the new jobs requires experience with prospects, incentives and contracts.

The seven elements of business development capacity build upon one another, and therefore should be considered sequential. There must be a significant level of capacity developed during work on the earlier elements in order to effectively proceed with the later elements in the process. For example, it generally makes very little sense for a community to invest significant resources in business recruitment marketing activities if it has virtually no available land and required infrastructure to offer.

Business Development Capacity Assessment

Within each of the seven elements of business development capacity is a series of factors that contribute to defining capacity. The seven elements are shown in shaded boxes, followed by their respective factors.

---

1. Business Development Strategy. A business development strategy, which can be viewed as a subset of a community and economic development strategy, should have a very clear scope. In addition to answering the question, "What types of business development activities should we engage in?" the strategy should be equally clear in identifying "What business development activities are beyond the scope of our community?" That is, many communities, due to limitations in factors such as workforce, proximity to markets, and available infrastructure, ought to conclude that the recruitment of large-scale business development opportunities is beyond the realistic grasp of the community.

Business development strategies should also assess the desirability of business growth within a community. Many urban and suburban cities experienced such dramatic growth in the 1990s that they became very selective about new job-creating possibilities. Times of economic recession cause communities to rethink these policies.

Often overlooked, and frequently most important, are activities to support existing businesses within a community. In the end, a large percentage of jobs created in any community will come from the expansion of existing businesses. Additionally, communities can often offset the threat of curtailment of business operations with proactive business retention efforts.

Communities must also assess the business development climate they offer. What is the condition of the state and national economy? How competitive is the state's business climate? How streamlined is the community's regulatory process for businesses?

1.a. Relationship with Community's Strategic Plan. If the community has developed a community strategic plan relative to its overall community and economic development needs, how does business development fit within that context? Is it a priority? Are there specific business development objectives?

1.b. Desirability of Business Development. For communities to successfully engage in business development activities, they must first have a broad desire, if not hunger, to pursue such activities. If a community has experienced recent rapid growth, the need to focus on growth management activities may trump the desire to pursue business development. In such a circumstance, the community will need, at a minimum, to sharpen its focus on the specific types of business development activities that remain especially appealing and are needed.

Still other communities, even without having experienced recent rapid growth, may not want to engage in business development activities. These communities may view themselves as a "bedroom community to a larger area," or simply a location that wishes to remain free from any of the effects of growth and business development that may result from such activities.

1.c. Appropriateness of Business Development. Regardless of the community's desire for growth, there are factors—many of which are uncontrollable or slow to change—that affect the ability of the community to succeed with business development strategies. Factors such as the location of the community, access to markets, available labor force, available infrastructure and the business climate of the state have a significant effect on a community's ability to engage in business development activities.

1.d. Foundation of Support for and from Existing Businesses. A high percentage of job-creating opportunities in any community comes from the existing business base. What efforts has the community made to better understand the current conditions and needs of existing businesses? Do these businesses feel a high level of support from local government and community leaders? Is there a concerted effort to systematically contact existing businesses? What might be the ultimate consequences if someone representing an existing business met with an executive of a company considering expanding into the community?

> **2. Local Staff and Team Development.** Similar to the community development capacity requirements, business development requires strong staffing, organization and volunteers in order to succeed. Communities must be careful not to assume that simply because they have broader community development organizations in place (that advocates for community livability, tourism development, downtown development, historic preservation, arts and culture and/or other priorities), that they have a business development organization. Business development can be coordinated through an organization with broader purposes but in order for it to be effective, specific skills and focus are necessary and cannot be diluted or lost.

2.a. Focused Business Development Organization. Successful business development, like all other community development opportunities, requires vision, focus and discipline. Communities must not only have a clear vision of their desired outcomes, but they must commit the resources of an organization toward the achievement of that vision.

Chambers of Commerce, for example, may or may not have a business development focus. Although their mission statement may directly include support for existing businesses, communities should examine the specific activities of their chamber to determine if all the necessary business development objectives are being adequately and competently pursued by the organization.

Are all of the necessary business development activities being clearly advanced by one or more development organization(s)? Is there an organization in the community whose sole purpose it is to engage in business development activities (this may not be necessary or affordable in some communities)? Does the organization have a broader mission, the pursuit of which dilutes its business development effectiveness? Does business development remain a priority, even with other community priorities vying for attention and resources?

2.b. Business Development Organization Stability. It is essential that the organization dedicated to advancing business development priorities has a stable base from which to operate. First and foremost, the community should ensure that funding provisions are in place for the business development organi
zation. Is the funding stable enough so the organization is not preoccupied with "keeping the doors open" and having to spend unwarranted time and effort fundraising?

2.c. Frequency of Meetings. In addition to vision and focus on business development, one additional essential ingredient is necessary: effort. Business development is a long-term—and sometimes long-shot—activity. This is especially true for the work needed to recruit specific businesses. The community must consistently make disciplined efforts dedicated to its business development activities.

These efforts must almost always include regular meetings of the business development organization and/or its partners and allies. In general, activities engaged in weekly are proactive, activities engaged in monthly sustain the direction and activities engaged in quarterly or less can be reactive and ineffective.

2.d. Business Development Staff. A key factor in successful business development activities is the presence of at least one focused, professional staff person. Business development is a sophisticated process and requires the employment of an individual—typically full-time—to remain abreast of business development trends, opportunities, and professional business development training offerings.

2.e. Business Development Training. Business development training opportunities are available and valuable for communities truly focused and dedicated to creating results. It is essential for business development staff to remain abreast of trends, financial and technical resources and proven professional practices. Additionally, training of community volunteers can prove very beneficial. Such training is provided by the International Economic Development Council and many state economic development associations.

---

3. Industrial Land and Infrastructure. Many communities get geared up to conduct business development—and particularly business recruitment—activities without first conducting an objective analysis of the existing availability of land and infrastructure.

Frequently, communities confuse the availability of land "zoned industrial" with the true availability of land appropriate for business expansion and business recruitment endeavors. Simply because land exists does not mean it is for sale—or for sale at a competitive price. It does not mean the land is necessarily served by infrastructure or is served by specialized infrastructure required by a particular industry. And it does not mean that the land is clear from environmental constraints.

Indeed, the availability of land, or lack thereof, which is truly available, appropriate and competitive for business development uses is a significant advantage or disadvantage/constraint for a community.

Issues of land ownership must also be considered. Although the community may think it has land available, what really happens when the existing expanding business or the industrial prospect comes seriously knocking on the door? Will the price of the land suddenly escalate? Is the landowner truly motivated to sell? Is he/she legally empowered to sell?

Communities may wish to consider the public ownership of industrial land to ensure that the public interest, rather than an individual or corporation's private interest, dominates the motivations of a future transaction. Perhaps this public ownership is in place through a port, county, city or other public entity. Even if the land is publicly owned, does the public body have a strategy for its ultimate use?

3.a. Availability of Industrially Zoned Land. Does the community have land that is zoned industrial? Is the land available of adequate size and configuration to accommodate potential development?

3.b. Potential for Land. Even if a community does not have existing available land, the community may be able to "create" such land through appropriate zoning, infrastructure planning and environmental assessment efforts. These processes often can take between six months and two years. Nonetheless, the potential availability of land definitely increases the long-term chances for new business development.

3.c. Land Ownership. The ownership of the land, and indeed the motivation of the potential land seller, is a key factor in the real availability of industrially zoned land. Ideally, the community has control of land that is truly available, properly zoned, competitively priced, and served with the infrastructure consistent with the needs of expanding and prospective businesses.

3.d. Environmental Considerations. Even if available land exists, has adequate infrastructure, and has a motivated seller, environmental issues can prove to be paramount. Is the land a Greenfield (land without previous industrial or commercial use) or a Brownfield (former mill site or other industrial use)? Has an environmental assessment been conducted on the site? Did the environmental assessment conclude the land is not contaminated? If not, is there a specific set of recommendations and anticipated costs to effectively address and mitigate the environmental issues in a timely fashion?

3.e. Land Price. The price of land, particularly compared to the price of land in competitive communities, is a key consideration. Does the community have an accurate assessment of the price competitiveness of its land? Is land price a significant decision factor for the types of business development activities being sought and/or anticipated by the community?

3.f. Availability of Buildings. Approximately three-quarters of all business development leads are seeking the availability of an existing building. For many communities, their existing stock of industrial buildings is virtually 100% utilized. Therefore, communities that have one or more available existing industrial building(s) may have a competitive advantage over other communities.

Because companies generally have detailed specifications for buildings, communities must also consider the desirability of their buildings. Do the existing buildings meet current code requirements? Are they of adequate size, including needed ceiling height? What is the condition of the existing buildings? Is there sufficient adjacent land for building expansion? Are the buildings competitively priced?

3.g. Basic Infrastructure. Industrial land must be served—or have the potential to be served within a short period (preferably no more than six months)—by basic infrastructure such as water, sanitary sewer, storm sewer, power and natural gas (if locally available). Communities frequently underestimate the cost of extending infrastructure to industrial sites. If infrastructure does not currently exist to an industrial site, the community can accelerate its development by conducting up-front planning, cost assessment and preliminary dialogue with potential infrastructure funding sources.

3.h. Access Infrastructure. Typically, the term "infrastructure" refers to sewer, water and other forms of *basic* infrastructure such as roads, rail and air transportation. For the purposes of this discussion, they are separated into basic, access and special infrastructure. At a minimum, industrial sites must be accessible via streets and roads. Ideally, the community provides immediate accessibility (within five minutes) to an interstate highway system. Additional modes of transportation, including rail, barging and air, can also prove critical in specific cases. The community should give consideration to the relative importance of various modes of transportation to the specific objectives of the business development activity.

3.i. Special Infrastructure. In addition to basic and access infrastructure, certain existing businesses and industrial prospects require special infrastructure such as fiber optic cable service, very large, cost-competitive quantities of electricity and immediate proximity to an international airport. (Obviously, the relative importance of special infrastructure varies significantly with the types of businesses considered as targets by the community.)

3.j. Land/Target Compatibility. Most industrial land is compatible with most business development opportunities. Nonetheless, a community that truly has targeted business development opportunities may be aware of special land and infrastructure requirements necessary to facilitate successful business development. Some industrial targets require, for example, a campus-like setting. Other businesses may have huge land configuration requirements (for logistics/distribution centers and high technology businesses, for example).

4. Targeted Industries. Similar to communities focusing on specific objectives included in their strategic plan, communities must also focus on their business development activities in order to be successful. The concept of "targeted industries" is the most often used procedure to identify, on a selective basis, the types of industry consistent with the development and recruitment desires of a particular community.

Typically, businesses are targeted based on the type of industry they represent as categorized in the North American Industry Classification System (NAICS). This system replaced the U.S. Standard Industrial Classification (SIC) system. There are additional methods for targeting industries that can be used either in addition to, or to replace, the industry selection process. Communities may target industries based upon a geographic region or upon other factors such as the size of typical companies. Communities may wish to begin their Targeted Industry Analysis by analyzing the types of companies that could locate in their community to produce products that are typically imported into the community. That is, they can substitute the local manufacturing of goods and services that have historically been imported. This is a process known as "import substitution."

Still other communities may wish to conduct their Targeted Industry Analysis to be consistent with other objectives and priorities. For example, communities that have historic strength—or current strategies—to expand the visitor industry, may wish to recruit businesses consistent with this focus.

Targeted Industry Analysis is a very sophisticated field, and communities can initiate fairly complex strategies and contract with specialized consultants to conduct such industry targeting.

4.a. Import Substitution. As defined immediately above, import substitution is the process of identifying goods and services that historically have been imported into the community, sometimes for further processing by existing manufacturing companies. If sufficient importing is occurring, it may "make the case" for the start-up, expansion or recruitment of a business that can manufacture these products locally. Simply by conducting an import substitution analysis, the community can become more familiar with its existing manufacturing base and set the stage for a more sophisticated business recruitment process.

4.b. Connection with the Strategic Plan. Ideally, a community's strategic planning process yields a clear understanding of the types of business development activities the community finds desirable. Does the community's strategic plan address the desirability of specific businesses and industries? If so, is this influencing the targeting of industries?

4.c. Targeted Industry Analysis. As indicated above, there are a variety of targeting techniques available. Most are centered on the identification of industries that are compatible with a community's desires and capacity for development. Has the community conducted a targeted-industry analysis? Was the analysis done with the assistance of trained professionals? Did the analysis yield a specific list of businesses to be contacted and cultivated?

5. Marketing. Once the business development strategy is in place, a local development team is poised, land and infrastructure is ready, and some level of Targeted Industry Analysis has been completed, the community is only then prepared to conduct specific business development marketing activities.

The sequential nature of the action elements of business development must be recognized. Conducting marketing activities without land to be offered is a waste of resources. Conducting a marketing strategy without some form of targeting, or market segmentation, can be very inefficient—if not completely unproductive.

The community needs to take a holistic, sophisticated approach to marketing techniques, perhaps including cold calling, direct mail, participation in industry trade shows, use of the Internet and establishing alliances with site selectors.

Finally, communities may wish to conduct business development–and, in particular, business recruitment–activities in concert with other communities and counties in their region. By conducting a regional approach, costs can be shared, and the possibility of attracting a company to the region increased.

5.a. Marketing Track Record. In many cases, communities have already conducted and/or are conducting business development marketing activities. An objective review of the results of these marketing activities should be done. What results have been generated by past and current marketing activities? These results can be measured and evaluated in terms of the total number of business leads generated, the total number of leads that resulted in companies that expressed a willingness to consider expansion or locating in the community, the total number of site visits generated, the number of companies actually expanding or locating in the community and finally, the number of jobs associated with companies that decided to expand or locate in the community.

A community should weigh these results against the long-shot nature of business development activity. It is generally accepted that between 1% and 5% of all business development leads actually result in success. If a community has a successful track record of business development marketing, it is poised for continued success. If past marketing activities have not been successful, communities can still learn from what worked—and didn't work.

5.b. Professional Marketing Assistance. The use of professional assistance in developing and implementing a business development marketing strategy can be an effective use of resources. Companies that have expertise in developing and implementing business development plans can eliminate much of the guesswork about what might work and what is certain to fail.

Communities, however, must be careful about turning all business development marketing activities over to the professionals. At a minimum, communities must develop a clear vision of the outcomes they are trying to achieve, and they must assign specific responsibilities to marketing professionals.

5.c. Diversification of Marketing Techniques. Consistent with the principles of business diversification, communities may wish to engage in a variety of business development marketing techniques to increase the likelihood of success.

Business development marketing techniques include cold calling, direct mail, participation in trade shows, use of the Internet and establishing alliances with site selectors. A history of business development activities will help a particular community hone in on successful techniques. Until this is done, using a more diversified set of marketing techniques can be effective and instructive.

5.d. Financial Resources. Perhaps more than any other factor in business development marketing, the availability of financial resources—that is, a funded budget—is essential. Marketing is expensive. It frequently takes repeated exposure to potential decision makers to successfully reach the desired market(s).

There is no certain formula to determine the correct amount of funding for business development marketing. The funds needed depend upon the marketing technique(s) utilized, the duration of the marketing campaign and the level of quality desired.

5.e. Use of the Internet. Today, the Internet is used almost universally for advertising, sales and related communications, including business development.

Companies can research business expansion possibilities and options in communities and at other locations simply by going online. Regularly, communities are evaluated without having any idea they may be under consideration for a possible business investment deal.

Similarly, communities can broadcast the availability of their land, buildings, workforce, infrastructure and incentives to a worldwide market at virtually no cost.

Communities must be able to utilize the Internet to make a positive first impression on business prospects and to cultivate business development leads.

---

6. Prospect and Lead Management. All of the activities described thus far in this business development capacity assessment section are designed to ultimately generate business development leads or prospects (these terms are used interchangeably here, although "prospect" is frequently used when the relationship between a community and a company is more specific and developed).

Businesses can take two years—or more—to make a business location decision based upon contacts they make with communities and the site information they receive. Generally, however, the decision process takes between six and twelve months. Regardless of the duration of this period, communities must be prepared to address each and every concern and need of a prospect.

Business development—and particularly business recruitment—is a process of elimination. Companies come to their ultimate site decision through a process of eliminating other communities that have one or more significant variances from the ideal conditions being sought by the company. Given this, communities must manage prospects by carefully and accurately answering every request for information.

Prospect management requires a very steady, professional approach to businesses. The efforts of a strong network of civic advocates in combination with the work of a well-trained business development professional maximize the likelihood of business development success.

6.a. Community Profile. One of the essential tools each community must prepare is a community profile. This document should be designed to answer virtually every basic question a business may ask.

At a minimum, the community profile should contain demographic data describing the community in terms of population, labor force, access to markets, availability and cost of infrastructure, educational facilities/programs and job training services. This information should be less than two years old, especially the demographic data that changes annually. A good community profile also provides information describing the community's quality of life and available commercial/industrial land and buildings, and related infrastructure. Ideally, the community profile can be accessed on-line.

6.b. A Professional Community Response. Business location decision makers have a very complex decision to make. In order to make a location decision that will have long-term, positive financial impacts for their corporation, they need information that is complete and accurate. Accordingly, they rely on a community to be prompt and thorough in its response.

Does the community have the capability of providing answers on a prompt and thorough basis? Are the internal relationships within the community working smoothly (among local government, utilities, employers, employment services, educational providers, etc.)? Is the community prepared to "drop everything" to respond to an immediate need for information? Is a coordinated business response team in place that represents all of the relevant entities listed above?

6.c. Availability to Travel. Although the need is infrequent, communities must be prepared to travel to a prospect company's headquarters to make their case. This need typically only develops when a community becomes a finalist in the site decision competition process. Communities must have the appropriate people, typically the staff professional and perhaps two other community leaders, and the funds necessary to finance the trip.

7. Closing the Deal. All prior steps in this business development capacity assessment mean virtually nothing if the community is not capable of "closing the deal." Generally, closing the deal is the process of eliminating any remaining uncertainties in the minds of the prospect company's decision makers. Almost always, these details—as well as the overall commitment by all parties (the company, the community, the state, and possibly other entities)—are formalized in a contract or memorandum of understanding.

Communities, therefore, have to be willing to put their commitment in writing. Both the company and the community may have to back up their commitment with potential penalties in the event that either party does not perform as agreed. Typically, performance from a community would be the guarantee of the delivery of land, infrastructure and local incentives. Communities, and particular the state, typically require a guarantee from the company to create the number and types of jobs negotiated in the site location process.

It is typical—and preferable from the state's perspective— for the topic of incentives to be seriously discussed late in the site location process. Companies that insist upon detailed incentive commitments early in the process may have the importance of incentives out of balance with respect to other site location factors (access to markets, cost of labor, etc.) Nonetheless, incentives of some form almost always become a required provision of the memorandum of understanding.

7.a. Deal-making Experience. Communities that have a track record of closing deals have gained invaluable experience. They tend to have greater intuition regarding the factors that are truly critical in the siting process. They may have relationships with the state, the attorney general's office and other players critical to closing deals.

7.b. Expertise with Incentives. Usually, it is only during the latter stages of the business recruitment process that a detailed discussion about incentives is required. Communities with expertise related to the availability and packaging of business development incentives—particularly from a staff person—have an edge over the competition. Communities that develop a strong partnership approach with the state also have an edge.

7.c. A Winning Attitude. Although it is intangible, and often hard to quantify, a winning attitude, one that reflects the idea that the project is destined to happen in the community, yields results. Such an attitude can be strengthened through an unbeatable internal team within the community (especially, government leaders, business executives, and community advocates). Typically, a community has a winning attitude or it does not. There is very little, if any, middle ground.

7.d. Community Sophistication. As indicated above, almost all business development siting processes culminate in a memorandum of understanding. Does the community have its own city attorney skilled in negotiating agreements? If not, is an attorney available to assist in the negotiation process?

7.e. Project/Contract Monitoring. Assuming that a successful business development deal culminates in an agreement, does the community have the sophistication to monitor the agreement to ensure compliance? Is the community able to meet all of its obligations?

COMMUNITY DEVELOPMENT CAPACITY

While there are dozens of factors that contribute to the capacity of a community to define and implement community development strategies, they can be categorized into seven distinct elements. The seven elements of Community Development Capacity are:

- Experience with Strategic Planning

- Project and Issue Advocacy

- Active, Effective Organization

- Capable, Professional Staffing

- Dedicated Community Volunteers

- Community Attitude

- Balance between Project and Community Advocacy

Element One: Experience with Strategic Planning. A common vision for the future backed by a plan to achieve the vision is a powerful instrument, especially if it is understood and supported by the citizenry. Past experience with creating and implementing such a plan is important.

Element Two: Project and Issue Advocacy. A plan for the future quickly becomes irrelevant if successful and continuing implementation of projects and addressing of relevant issues do not support it.

Element Three: Active, Effective Organization. It takes an organization focused on the implementation of the strategic plan to consistently advocate for priority projects and to effectively address issues.

Element Four: Capable, Professional Staffing. Community development is a profession. It is essential that capable people be in the right positions to serve the community.

Element Five: Dedicated Community Volunteers. While capable professional staff people are essential, they need the support and active involvement of the citizenry to be effective.

Element Six: Community Attitude. Communities have a collective attitude about their future. This attitude can either support or hinder community development capacity.

Element Seven: Balance between Project and Community Advocacy. Project and issue proponents must keep in mind that their agenda is a subset of the overall direction of the community.

Community Development Capacity Assessment

Within each of the seven elements of Community Development Capacity are a series of factors that contribute to defining capacity.

> **1. Experience with Strategic Planning.** Communities are in various stages of commitment to a strategic planning process. Some communities have never engaged in such an effort to collectively envision the future and set specific projects in motion to realize that vision. Conversely, others not only have a strategic planning process in place, but have enlisted professional strategic planning consultants in the effort, have enjoyed robust citizen participation in the development of the plan, have reviewed it regularly and may have updated the plan one or more times.

1.a. Existence of Community-wide Strategic Planning Document. The mere fact that a community has completed some form of community-wide strategic planning process generally shows that it realizes it can take charge of its future. Ideally, the strategic planning process is broad in scope, inclusive of the entire community, thorough in its identification of strengths/weaknesses/opportunities/threats of the community, specific in its conclusions and recommendations, prescriptive in identifying "who is to do what by when" and visionary in its overall recommendations.

1.b. Acceptance of Plan. In order for the strategic plan to be ultimately effective, it must be accepted by the elected officials of the community (typically the city council or county commission). Plan acceptance can occur either by formal resolution or simply through passive awareness and acceptance.

1.c. Professional Development of Plan. Professional organizations and consultants skilled in conducting strategic planning services are available to communities.

Advantages of professional strategic planning services include the utilization of proven processes, the objectivity of an outside facilitator, connection with external strategic planning resources and the professionalism of the final, written product.

1.d. Use of the Strategic Plan. The ultimate test of the strategic planning process is the use of the final product itself. At best, a strategic plan has the potential to impact a community and its leadership structure at a very deep and personal level. Ultimately, community leaders can all be "singing off the same song sheet" in support of broad community advancements, all articulated in the strategic plan. At worst, the strategic plan becomes the proverbial "report on the shelf" that never gets used.

1.e. Plan Updating. One of the truest tests of strategic planning is the overall value to the community. If the strategic planning process—and the plan itself—truly has value, then the community will be motivated to update it on a periodic basis (perhaps every three to five years). A strategic planning process that has been repeated on more than one occasion shows a true long-term commitment by a community to its future.

2. Project and Issue Advocacy. Typically, a strategic planning process yields an overall vision statement and a series of goals and objectives related to projects and issues. For the purposes of this evaluation tool, projects and issues are separated in the strategic planning process.

Ultimately, it is the success, or lack thereof, of a community in advancing projects and addressing issues that reinforces its commitment to long-term strategic planning. Communities must experience this "pay-off" to reinforce a long-term outlook.

2.a. Community Wish List. At a minimum, many communities have established a "wish list" of desirable projects. This list does not necessarily imply that the community has identified the necessary steps and resources to complete projects. It is evidence, however, that the community has taken a collective approach to considering its short- and long-term needs.

2.b. Identification of Strategic Issues. Frequently, issues of regional significance beyond the borders of a community impact the community. These issues can relate to the use of public lands, transportation access, workforce quality, human services, telecommunications and other concerns. Communities that not only recognize these broader issues, but also begin to form partnerships with other communities and regional organizations, have enhanced community development capacity.

2.c. Large Project Advocacy. Virtually every community has a short list of fairly significant, big-ticket projects that need advancement for the general welfare of the community. Frequently, these projects are infrastructure projects such as citywide improvements to sewer and water systems. In other cases, the community is seeking large-scale community facility improvements such as community centers, senior centers and health and wellness facilities. It requires significant community capacity to not only identify these projects, but to effectively advocate for the technical and financial assistance to carry them through to fruition.

2.d. Coordinating Projects with State and Federal Processes. Over time, communities develop the relationships and skills necessary to advance priorities in broader contexts. Communities must advance projects and issues in processes governed by state and federal agencies, for example.

2.e. Incorporated into Community Facilities Plan. Many states require cities to complete a community facilities plan. The facilities plan should comprehensively consider a city's facilities requirements, including its water system, sewer system and other public facilities. Communities enhance their capacity for project implementation by coordinating the required community facilities plan with all the other community development priorities.

3. Active, Effective Organization. Strategic planning and project identification means very little to a community if it does not have the organizational capacity to carry out the city's priorities. Although there is not "one correct way" to organize a community to conduct community development activities, there are some basic principles that apply. First of all, the scope of the community development activities needs to be defined. Communities may desire to implement projects and address issues that deal with the following types of community development activities: tourism development, historic preservation, arts and culture development, infrastructure improvements and community facilities. A community's priority list may be even longer.

A community may seek to empower one organization to advance the full gamut of community development priorities. Conversely, it may decide to have more than one organization (a visitor and convention bureau, a downtown development association, a business recruitment organization, etc.) focus on specific priorities. The process used by the community to determine how to structure and establish community development organization(s) should primarily be driven by the need to accomplish the work in its strategic plan, rather than beginning with a particular type of organization in mind.

This process advances, therefore, the following principles for a community's "organizational structure:"
- A community must have one or more organization(s) dedicated to advancing specific priorities identified in the strategic plan.
- If a community has more than one organization serving a community development advocacy role, the organizations must avoid duplication of services and reinforce each other.
- The organization(s) should have adequate, stable funding and dedicate a majority of their time to reaching stated objectives rather than simply keeping the organization(s) afloat.
- The organization(s) must meet frequently enough to advance identified priorities.

3.a. Connectedness and Focus of Organization(s). As indicated earlier, strategic planning and project development are essential elements of community development capacity. Typically, it falls to an appropriate community development organization(s) to implement the identified priorities of the community. It is necessary, therefore, for such an organization(s) to be connected to the plans and be conducting the activities prescribed in them. In effect, the organization(s) must be clearly aligned with the direction the community is pursuing.

3.b. Organizational Stability. It is essential that the organization(s) dedicated to advancing community development priorities has a stable structure and operations but is flexible enough to adjust to emerging and intensifying priorities.

First and foremost, the community should examine the funding provisions in place for the community development organization(s). Is the organization(s) funded through a dedicated source (consistent commitment through a city/county/port general fund?

dedicated use of lottery funding? consistent support from transient room tax? etc.)? Communities typically would never question the need to maintain adequate police, fire and street funding. Where does the community's commitment to funding community development stand in this context?

3.c. Focus on Business of Community. A community development organization can either be proactively involved in advocating for the priorities of its community, or it can react to the "crisis de jour." Is the organization's agenda consistent from meeting to meeting, reflecting a consistent focus on priorities, or does the agenda change with the whims of external forces? Does the organization have a track record of successes before beginning to advance new priorities?

3.d. Frequency of Meetings. The frequency of meetings can have a direct impact on the ability of projects to succeed and organizations to thrive. Successful work on large-scale projects may require meetings as frequently as once-per-week for periods stretching for one or more years. Community-based organizations with community-wide agendas typically need to meet at least monthly in order to successfully carry out their project(s). Additionally, community-wide organizations may need active subcommittees that meet between these regular meetings in order to pursue specific objectives. Organizations that meet on an "as-needed" basis (typically quarterly) are reactionary, and are generally not as effective.

3.e. Organizational Board Training. Increasingly, training is becoming available for community leaders who give their time and talent to specific boards and commissions. Communities enhance their community development capacity by providing training for these volunteers so they have a greater context for the work they are doing and are up-to-date regarding tools available to them.

---

4. Capable, Effective Staffing. For community development organizations to reach optimal effectiveness, a professional staff person must serve them. Community development organization staffing requires a talented individual (or team of individuals), strong staff support, a connection to organizational objectives and long-term staff training and development.

4.a. Skill Level of Staff Person. Perhaps more than any other single element, the skill level of the community development staff person can make or break a community development effort. Skills include basics such as written and oral communication, interpersonal skills and simply the overall competence of the individual. Also significant is the network the staff person has established and can draw upon as a result of years working in the field.

4.b. Support Staff. Communities of approximately 5,000 population and greater may find that their community development staff person has a work load that requires administrative support. Support staff can be part-time, and primarily serves to maximize the performance of the primary staff person.

4.c. Staff Focused on Organizational Objectives. As indicated earlier, community development organizations—and therefore the staff of these organizations—must spend a very high percentage of their time focused on the implementation of their priorities, not simply "keeping the organization afloat." As such, community development staff professionals should spend only a small portion of their time raising funds.

4.d. Staff Training. Community development staff can take advantage of training opportunities that are offered at the regional, state and even national levels. This training can be general (such as time and personnel management) or very specific (such as instruction on economic development techniques, programs and resources).

5. Dedicated Community Volunteers. Individuals are frequently motivated to commit their time and talent to their community because they understand the importance of contributing to a greater cause. Volunteers enjoy being a part of a "winning team" and desire to see their community succeed. Successful communities inspire civic volunteerism, and often reward volunteers for their time and service.

5.a. Opportunities for Service. The process of envisioning, planning and enacting community development activities offers significant opportunities for volunteerism. Communities that foster and promote the resulting volunteer opportunities and positions are most likely to reach their civic potential.

5.b. Celebration of Volunteerism. Traditionally, Chambers of Commerce hold annual luncheons or banquets during which they typically celebrate and recognize the "Persons of the Year" and "Businesses of the Year," as well as achievements in other categories of excellence. For many volunteers, this is the only recognition they receive other than the intrinsic reward of serving others.

6. Community Attitude. Although intangible, the attitude of a community is a major element in its capacity for community development. Like individuals, communities can be either proactive or reactive. They can believe they are in charge of their destiny or that there are too many uncontrollable factors or forces to make proactive behavior worth the effort.

Success is contagious. So is failure. Communities that have established a track record of envisioning and completing community development projects believe their next success is just around the corner. Communities that have tried and failed—or have not tried at all—do not sense they control their destiny. It's all about attitude.

6.a. Proactive versus Reactive Communities. Proactive communities envision the future and make it happen. They are very specific about defined outcomes and realize it is only a matter of time until they achieve success. Reactive communities find that their agenda—if they have one at all—is often compromised by external forces such as new state and federal regulations.

6.b. Viewing the Glass Half Full. Perception is reality. If a community believes it has a successful community development game plan and track record, it generally does—and will. For example, a community can choose to view its unemployment rate as either 30% above the national average (half- empty) or 10% lower than it was three years ago (half-full).

---

7. Balance between Project and Community Advocacy. A community completes a strategic planning exercise. The exercise yields a series of community development projects. Local organizations, equipped with staff and volunteers, focus on the implementation of the strategic projects. How does the community, at this point, view the importance of the projects? Do the projects become of paramount importance over the broader, strategic direction of the community? Or do civic leaders maintain the appropriate perspective of successful projects fitting into the broader community development vision?

Ideally, civic leaders will view their efforts to advance projects in the broader context. Even the chairperson for the largest community development project should view that project as subordinate to the community's strategic plan.

7.a. Commitment to Strategic Direction. In order for project proponents to view their project in the broader community context, they need to know the direction of the community itself. Advocates for an industrial park, for example, may be out of tune with the leadership of the community that prefers more of a Bedroom Community Development strategy, which would likely minimize the desirability for industrial recruitment. It is therefore beneficial for communities to have an identifiable strategic direction with clear objectives. Understanding of the strategic direction by the general citizenry is also important.

7.b. Subordination of Projects to Community. At a minimum, project advocates should see their project in the broader community context. They should view themselves as a part of a "fraternity of projects" advocating to advance the community. Advocates of specific projects should not view themselves as competitors with other community projects.

At a maximum, the community may wish to take some formal steps to build "teams of projects" that all subordinate themselves to the community's overall direction. Community-wide organizations such as Chambers of Commerce, progress boards or economic development organizations may want to take the lead in this endeavor.

THE TIMING OF CHANGING CIVIC CAPACITY FACTORS
Of all of the aspects of community and economic development, civic capacity is the most easily shaped by a community (think of it as watering your Two-Fruited Tree). Communities can invest in the human, financial and technical capacity of their community. Building local capacity, therefore, is one of the most "controllable" aspects of community and economic development.

Virtually everything in terms of hiring staff, training people, building volunteer organizations, committing funding and designing marketing campaigns can be initiated and concluded within two years.

Compare this to the similar "change time" in Chapter Five (Civic Strategies and Initiatives). As noted in that discussion on Key Success Factors related to implementing specific strategies, only 22 of the 88 factors (25 percent) can be changed in less than one year. Of the 66 business development Key Success Factors that take more than a year to change, about half of them can be influenced in one-to-five years, and the rest take five years or more, if they can be influenced at all.

In short, civic capacity, unlike civic condition and the Key Success Factors for implementing strategies, is very malleable. Combined with healthy civic condition (achievement and actualization motivations), communities can set the stage for progress.

> ### From Civic Capacity to Strategies and Initiatives
>
> Next, we shift to the ultimate objective of all community and economic development efforts: setting the stage to create jobs and improve the community's quality of life. These are the two fruits on the Two-Fruited Tree.
>
> Chapter Five puts strategy into strategic planning. After civic condition has been assessed, and civic capacity determined and improved, the proactive work needed to define the plan begins.
>
> Chapter Five presents the universe of community and economic development strategies, as well as a listing of many of the most popular quality-of-life initiatives. The strategic selection of strategies and initiatives is the make-or-break moment for defining the future of communities.

CHAPTER FIVE
Civic Strategies and Initiatives

CHAPTER FIVE
Civic Strategies and Initiatives

When people think about community and economic development, they ultimately have one or both of two outcomes in mind for their community: a stronger and more diversified economy and improved quality of life. These are the two "fruits" of community and economic development activities.

In general, business development strategies lead to economic benefits, while community development strategies produce quality-of-life enhancements. A bubble chart that presents the relative economic and quality-of-life benefits is shown later in this chapter.

For a community to truly be strategic about its future, it must set itself on a course that will ultimately succeed. In order to do this, it must select strategies that: 1) build upon comparative advantages, 2) are desired by the people of the community and 3) are supported by the capacity (Chapter Four) to implement the strategies.

Getting back to our Two-Fruited Tree, the process of selecting strategies is represented by the annual spring formation of the buds on a tree. The buds are not yet the fruit but they represent the potential benefits the tree will yield in the months ahead. Just as the buds of the tree will yield fruit consistent with the characteristics of the tree, the community must examine its characteristics to determine which fruit (strategies and initiatives) it can produce.

The Strategy Wheel™ on the previous page presents the 25 strategic options—strategies—from which communities can select and implement to strengthen and diversify their local economy and improve their quality of life. The strategies can be grouped into three major categories: business development strategies, community development strategies and other strategies. Likewise, the business development strategies can be grouped into four sub-categories: general, sector-specific, value-added and tourism development.

Of these strategies, what should a community select? What buds should form?

First and foremost, a community should strategically select strategies that build upon its strengths. Why select Value-added Agriculture in a region that has no real capacity to produce agricultural commodities, for example? Why select Destination Tourism in a community that has nothing of interest to offer tourists?

To avoid such inappropriate choices, *Key Success Factors* need to be considered. For the 25 strategies, there are a combined 88 Key Success Factors—conditions or abilities necessary for the successful implementation of one or more strategies. To be strategic, therefore, means to do an objective analysis based on these factors. The result will be a priority list of the 25 strategies on one of the three major decisions determinates (what a community *should* do based upon likelihood of success. The other two determinates are what the community *wants* to do and what the community *can* do based upon its capacity to implement its plan).

Figure 1 is a graphical depiction of the likelihood of successful implementation for the 25 strategies for a hypothetical community. Spokes of longer length represent strategies with a greater chance of generating positive results. Strategies such as Entrepreneurial Development, Energy Development, Value-added Forest Products, Value-Added Fisheries, Cultural Tourism, Health Care Expansion and Attracting Funding have Key Success Factors of relative strength. Strategies such as Business Recruitment, Business Cultivation, Logistics Center, Leading-edge Development, Bedroom Community Development, Attracting Lone Eagles and Attracting Retirees have Key Success Factors of relative weakness.

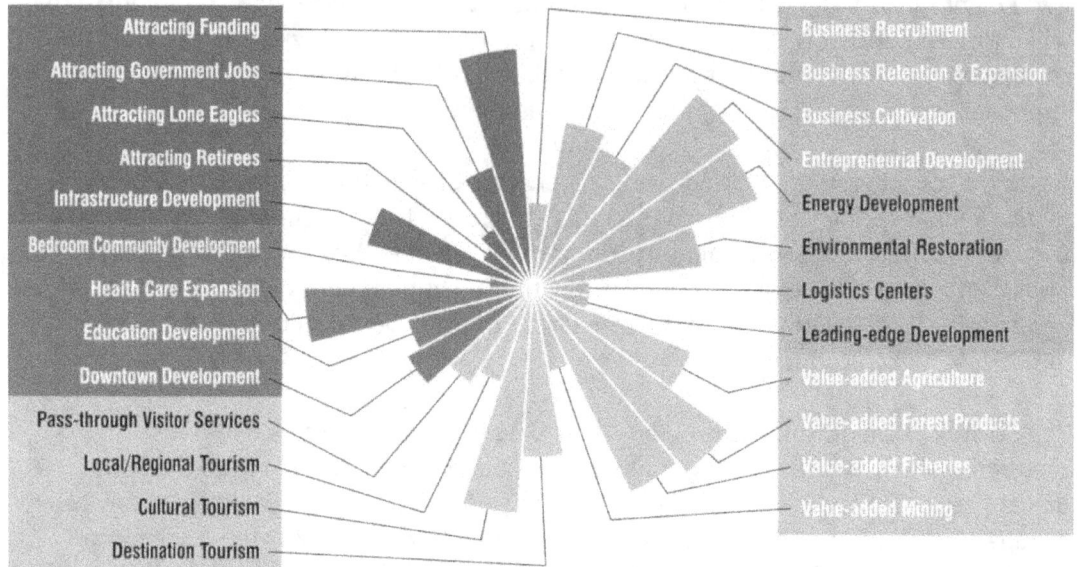

Attracting Funding	Business Recruitment
Attracting Government Jobs	Business Retention & Expansion
Attracting Lone Eagles	Business Cultivation
Attracting Retirees	Entrepreneurial Development
Infrastructure Development	Energy Development
Bedroom Community Development	Environmental Restoration
Health Care Expansion	Logistics Centers
Education Development	Leading-edge Development
Downtown Development	Value-added Agriculture
Pass-through Visitor Services	Value-added Forest Products
Local/Regional Tourism	Value-added Fisheries
Cultural Tourism	Value-added Mining
Destination Tourism	

Figure 1

There are 88 Key Success Factors relevant to one or more of the 25 strategies. The factors can be grouped into seven categories: Assets, Capital, Expertise, Government, Infrastructure, Land and Location.

Assets

For many strategies, communities must possess or have proximity to very specific assets. These assets range from proximity to certain raw materials, to availability of visitor attractions, to the existence of current business activity and to very broad quality-of life conditions.

> **Assets**
> ...are industry- or activity-specific conditions or dynamics critical to the success of many strategies.

This assets category is the broadest of the seven groups of Key Success Factors, and is a catch-all category for a broad range of factors. Nonetheless, the possession or proximity to these assets is a make-or-break for many strategies. Key Success Factors relevant to this category include:

- Availability of energy resources

- Availability of urban services

- Available, desirable housing

- Desirable climate

- Existing recreational amenities

- Existing or prospective cultural attraction

- Expandable educational institution

- Financially sound existing health care facility

- Insulation from industrial business annoyances

- Local recreational and visitor attractions

- Proximity and access to forests and forest products

- Proximity to fisheries commodities

- Proximity to large volumes of agricultural commodities

- Proximity to nationally recognized attractions

- Proximity to raw materials and minerals

- Proximity to travel routes

- Proximity to urban population and workforce centers

- Quality residential neighborhoods

- Recognizable central business district/downtown

- Sufficient base of local businesses

- Sufficient local entrepreneurial base

Capital

Access to—and consistent availability of—capital is significant in two general respects. First, businesses must be able to secure sufficient debt and/or equity capital for their formation, operations, retention and expansion. Second, development organizations must have reliable sources of funding in order to regularly engage in activities consistent with their mission.

> **Capital**
> ...represents business debt and equity funding, as well as consistent funding for development organizations to succeed.

For businesses, access to capital is the lifeblood of the business itself. For small businesses that can demonstrate loan repayment capability, programs to provide such capital can be very traditional (bank and credit union lending), or they can be government supported loan, loan guarantee or credit enhancement measures designed to supplement traditional lending.

For development organizations, reliable funding is necessary so the board and staff primarily engage in activities consistent with the organizational mission, rather than regularly chasing funding sources for the preservation of the organization itself.

- Ability to secure long-term contracts for forest materials

- Ability to secure power-purchase agreements

- Access to large-scale capital

- Access to long-term infrastructure loans and grants

- Access to small-business financing

- Availability of appropriated funds

- Competitive recruitment incentives

- Dedicated local financial resources for staffing recruiters

- Local funding for downtown development

- Sufficient marketing, promotion or public relations budget

Expertise

In this information age, it should be no surprise that one of the broadest and most important categories of Key Success Factors is expertise. The successful implementation of virtually every strategy requires expertise by a broad array of professionals in any community.

> **Expertise**
> ...includes the skills, connections and abilities of local professionals that can "make or break" many strategies.

Not only should expertise be possessed by the individuals on the front lines of community and business development, but such experience is also important in various professional sectors of the local economy, in the advancement of targeted tourism and downtown development strategies and in the ability of the professionals backing up the front-line community and business developers (city managers, public works directors, county commissioners, etc.).

Expertise is synonymous with professional capability referenced in the Four Stages of Civic Condition model. Key Success Factors relevant to this category include:

- Ability to build a team comprised of energy-development experts

- Ability to compete in a global market

- Ability to identify product and service gaps

- Ability to network and attend relevant trade shows

- Ability to successfully market value-added products

- Ability to understand industry trends and opportunities

- Accurate, long-term analysis of infrastructure needs and costs

- Capable, experienced economic development professionals

- Competent, strategic-minded hospital and health care executives

- Cooperation of economic development staff and educational community

- Cultural development and advocacy organization

- Dedicated business coaching staff

- Downtown organization and staff

- Existing excellence in local health care

- Implementation of national Main Street Four-Point Approach™

- Local ability to identify and advance a funding proposal

- Relationship with site selectors

- Relative sophistication in coordinating and marketing local events

- Sophisticated tourism development and promotion

- Sophisticated use of the Internet for marketing

- Staff focused on attracting retirees and/or lone eagles

- Support from local education professionals at all levels

- Supportive post-secondary education and training programs

- Team approach to financing infrastructure

Government

Increasingly, people argue that "if only government would get out of the way" our communities and businesses would thrive. In reality, however, it is through government (federal, state and especially local) that key strategies are envisioned, defined and enacted.

> **Government**
> ...provides many resources—and sets the tone—for many business and community development activities.

Governmental bodies not only establish policies and funding programs, but they also create cultures and attitudes that are either pro-development or anti-development. Strong collaboration between government and the private and volunteer sectors is an essential ingredient for success.

- Active engagement of downtown building and business owners

- Community acceptance of the visitor industry

- Community support for needed infrastructure rate increases

- Favorable state policies regarding office locations

- Local focus on revenues from visitors

- Local government support

- Local policies and ordinances supporting quality neighborhood development

- Local pro-business climate

- Projected growth in government budgets

- Strong community support

- Strong relations between economic development organization and local businesses

- Strong state and/or federal legislative delegation(s)

- Support for attracting retirees

- Support from local businesses

- Supportive state energy policies and incentives

Infrastructure

In order for communities to be attractive for many strategies, they must possess sufficient land, infrastructure, buildings and housing.

Here we use the term infrastructure very broadly (beyond just sewer, water and power facilities). Key Success Factors relevant to this category include:

> **Infrastructure**
> ...includes the land, buildings, housing, water systems, sewer systems, power facilities and other infrastructure necessary to advance many of the business development strategies.

- Adequate housing for labor force

- Adequate telecommunications infrastructure

- Availability of Brownfield sites

- Availability of industrially zoned land for industrial park development

- Availability of land for business prospects

- Availability of local buildings

- Availability of local infrastructure

- Excess water and sewer infrastructure capacity

- High-speed Internet

- Land/Buildings/Campus for education expansion

- Proximity to transmission lines with excess capacity

Labor

It takes a deeper bench than simply the "experts" to successfully implement many strategies. The availability and skills of the local labor force are critical to many strategies. Labor can be classified as high-skill and low-skill. Therefore, there are only two Key Success Factors for this category.

> **Labor**
> ...is the combination of the labor force and community volunteers who form the backbone of many business and community development activities.

- Available high-skill local labor pool
- Available low-skill local labor pool

Location

The location of the community is of great significance to many strategies. For example, communities that are strategically located to provide access to markets have a comparative advantage over relatively isolated communities.

> **Location**
> ...relates to certain strategies which must have access and/or proximity to people and/or markets in order to be successful.

Although it is generally agreed that advances in telecommunications capacity and capability now allow business activity to be conducted from anywhere, for many strategies the specific location of the community is still paramount. These location Key Success Factors include:

- Advantageous location for government or education expansion
- Prospect of an expanded geographic market for health care
- Proximity and access to markets
- Proximity to scheduled air service
- Strategic location for logistics center

THE TIMING OF CHANGING KEY SUCCESS FACTORS

Knowledgeable people in the field of community and economic development wisely counsel that communities should invest at least three years—and probably at least five—in their community and economic development program before expecting broad, measurable results. This is especially true with the business development strategies, most notably Business Recruitment.

Studying the "change time" of the Key Success Factors underscores this fact. The table below presents the typical period of time it would take a community to acquire a particular Key Success Factor if it did not initially possess it.

"Change Time" for Key Success Factors									
Category	Instant	< 3 Months	3-6 Months	6-12 Months	12-24 Months	2-5 Years	5-20 Years	Unchangeable	TOTAL
Assets	0	0	0	0	0	7	5	9	21
Capital	0	0	1	5	2	2	0	0	10
Expertise	0	0	1	13	9	0	1	0	24
Government	0	0	0	2	7	3	2	1	15
Infrastructure	0	0	0	0	0	8	2	1	11
Labor	0	0	0	0	0	0	2	0	2
Location	0	0	0	0	0	0	0	5	5
TOTAL	0	0	2	20	18	20	12	16	88

For example, of the 21 Asset Category Key Success Factors, nine of them are unchangeable. That is, if a community does not possess that particular factor now, there is no possibility that it will in the future either.

Only 22 of the 88 factors, 25 percent, can be changed in less than one year (and 20 of the 22 take at least six months of planning and concerted effort). Of the 66 factors that take more than a year to change, about half of them can be positively influenced in one-to-five years, and the rest take five years or more, if they can be influenced at all. Bottom line: community and economic development takes time. Only two of the seven categories, Capital and Expertise, have a majority of factors that can be shaped and acquired within a one year. Notably, it is these two categories that are most relevant to civic capacity. On the other end of the spectrum, the Assets and Location categories have a majority (or near majority) of unchangeable factors.

Compare this to the discussion at the end of Chapter Four. While the "change time" for Key Success Factors is relatively slow, the amount of time it takes to improve civic capacity (human, financial and technical resources), is comparatively fast. In other words, communities have more control over their capacity to implement community and economic development activities than they do the conditions that surround them. Ideally, communities take proactive measures on all factors relevant to successfully envisioning and enacting their future. It is said that "luck" is when opportunity meets preparation. If so, community and economic development takes preparation.

NOTE: Each of the 25 community and economic development strategies are presented below. In order to objectively evaluate the viability of each of the strategies for a given community, visit www.buildingcommunities.us/key-success-factor-analysis.html.

Business Recruitment

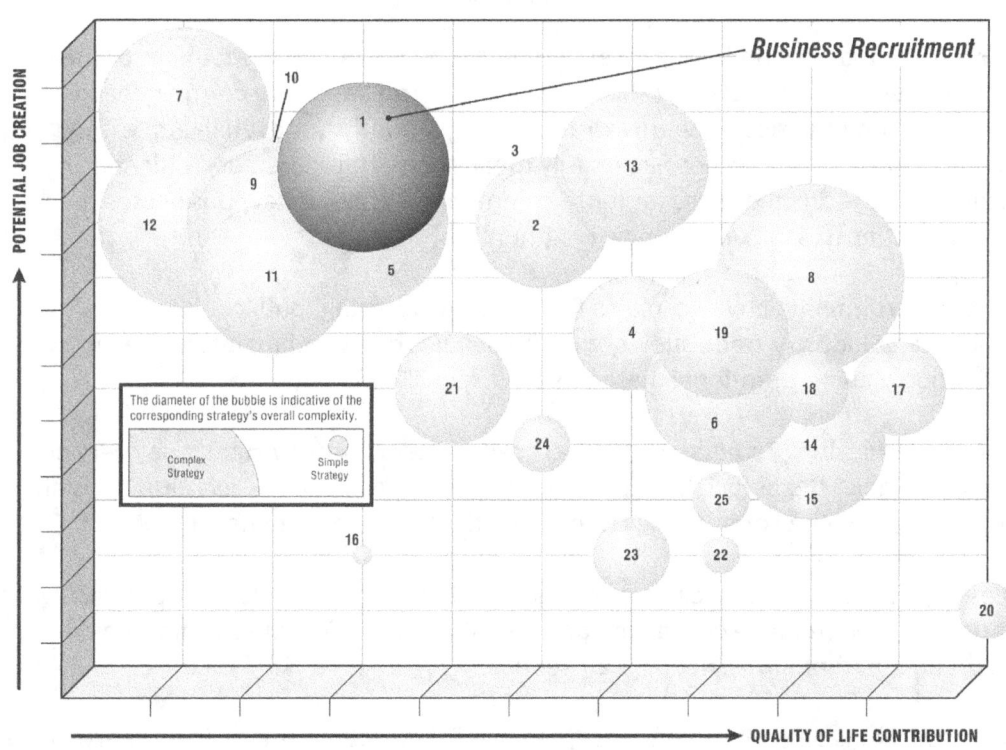

POTENTIAL JOB CREATION

Business Recruitment

The diameter of the bubble is indicative of the corresponding strategy's overall complexity.

Complex Strategy

Simple Strategy

QUALITY OF LIFE CONTRIBUTION

1. Business Recruitment
2. Business Retention & Expansion
3. Business Cultivation
4. Entrepreneurial Development
5. Energy Development
6. Environmental Restoration
7. Logistics Centers
8. Leading-edge Development
9. Value-added Agriculture
10. Value-added Forest Products
11. Value-added Fisheries
12. Value-added Mining
13. Destination Tourism
14. Cultural Tourism
15. Local/Regional Tourism
16. Pass-through Visitor Services
17. Downtown Development
18. Education Development
19. Health Care Expansion
20. Bedroom Community Development
21. Infrastructure Development
22. Attracting Retirees
23. Attracting Lone Eagles
24. Attracting Government Jobs
25. Attracting Funding

Business Recruitment

Perhaps the most widely recognized economic development strategy is business recruitment, which is the act of proactively soliciting existing businesses located outside a community to relocate or expand within it.

> **Business Recruitment**
> ...is a set of activities designed to attract businesses from outside the community to relocate or expand within it. The objective is to move existing jobs from one location to another, and perhaps simultaneously to increase the number of these jobs.

There are significant benefits to a community that successfully recruits new business activity to town. Jobs are created, the community's tax base is expanded, existing businesses may benefit and the news of the new business is a source of positive energy for the entire community.

However, business recruitment can have drawbacks. Communities that do not have the desire or infrastructure capacity for growth may view business recruitment negatively. Also, some existing business may be negatively impacted if a recruited new business is a competitor.

Communities that rely on business recruitment as a substantial component of their economic development strategy should view their effort as a long-term endeavor. Frequently, communities using this strategy can go months (or even years) without tangible results. This does not necessarily mean their efforts are poorly planned or executed. The fact is there are far more communities chasing new businesses than there are businesses looking for new communities.

Business recruitment activity can also be costly. Advertising, public relations, attendance at industry trade shows, website development and maintenance, and informational and promotional materials are expensive.

Communities desiring to pursue a business recruitment strategy should pay very close attention to all of the associated Key Success Factors. As business recruitment is highly competitive, only the communities that are at the top of their game will succeed.

Necessary keys to success include a sophisticated economic development team, a very competitive labor force, existing land and infrastructure, widespread community support and, potentially, scheduled air service.

One factor that is difficult to define is "patience." Communities may have everything in place and perpetually come in "runner up" on key business recruitment projects. If they are "runner up," this means that virtually all of the ingredients for success are in place. Perseverance then becomes an additional factor.

Recently, the terms "business recruitment" and "business attraction" have become interchangeable. While the terms generally refer to the same activity, it is possible and useful to separate them.

Business attraction refers to many actions a community can and should take in order to position itself more competitively for bringing new businesses to town. These efforts typically relate either to preparatory activities such as land and site development, streamlining codes and regulations and community clean-ups or marketing activities such as updating websites and producing new marketing pieces.

By comparison, business recruitment is more focused upon the back-end activities such as attending tradeshows, managing prospects and closing deals.

Business recruitment is clearly not for everyone. In addition to the existence—or lack thereof—of the associated Key Success Factors is the underlying desire of the community as a whole to pursue growth and physical expansion. Communities that have experienced growth may have a large constituency that has seen enough growth. The recruitment of new businesses, therefore, may need to provide benefits to the broader citizenry.

Examples of Strategic Implementation Activities

- Advertisement and public relations in industry periodicals
- Attendance at industrial tradeshows
- Business prospecting through relationships with site selectors
- Geographic-specific business prospecting
- Industry-specific business prospecting
- Relationship-based business prospecting

Advantages	Drawbacks
• Potential for substantial job creation • Family wage jobs • Expansion of local tax base • General enhancement of community vitality	• Communities that do not have the desire or infrastructure capacity for growth may view business recruitment negatively • Existing business may be negatively impacted

Key Success Factors

- Ability to network and attend relevant trade shows
- Ability to compete in a global market
- Access to large-scale capital
- Availability of local buildings
- Availability of local infrastructure
- Availability of local land
- Capable, experienced economic development professionals
- Competitive recruitment incentives
- Dedicated local financial resources for staffing recruiters
- Local government support
- Local, available, high-skill labor pool
- Local, available, low-skill labor pool
- Proximity and access to markets
- Proximity to scheduled air service
- Relationship with site selectors
- Sophisticated use of the Internet for marketing
- Strong community support
- Support from local businesses

Business Retention & Expansion

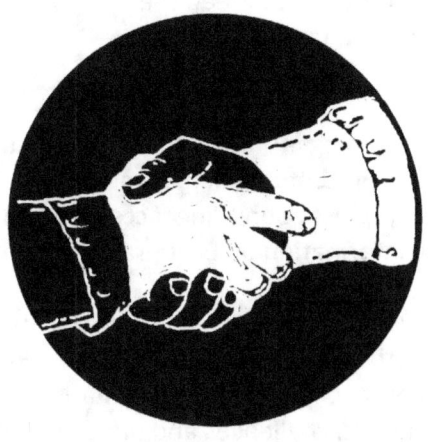

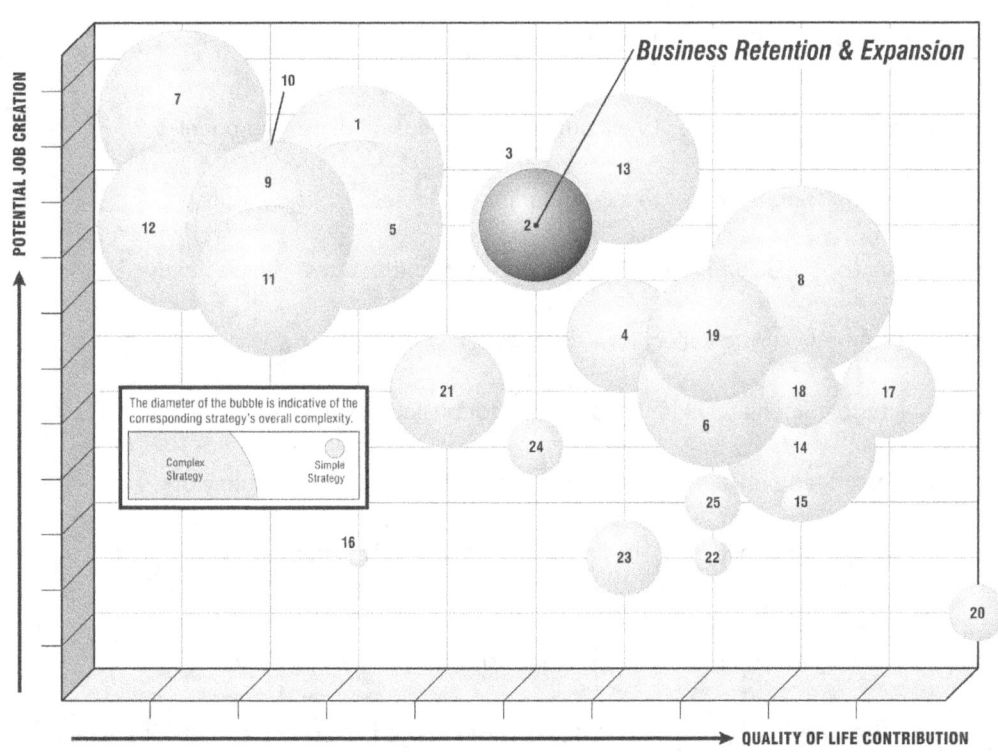

Business Retention & Expansion

POTENTIAL JOB CREATION

The diameter of the bubble is indicative of the corresponding strategy's overall complexity.

Complex Strategy

Simple Strategy

QUALITY OF LIFE CONTRIBUTION

1. Business Recruitment
2. Business Retention & Expansion
3. Business Cultivation
4. Entrepreneurial Development
5. Energy Development
6. Environmental Restoration
7. Logistics Centers
8. Leading-edge Development
9. Value-added Agriculture
10. Value-added Forest Products
11. Value-added Fisheries
12. Value-added Mining
13. Destination Tourism
14. Cultural Tourism
15. Local/Regional Tourism
16. Pass-through Visitor Services
17. Downtown Development
18. Education Development
19. Health Care Expansion
20. Bedroom Community Development
21. Infrastructure Development
22. Attracting Retirees
23. Attracting Lone Eagles
24. Attracting Government Jobs
25. Attracting Funding

Business Retention & Expansion

It is widely agreed by most economic development professionals that opportunities for job retention and expansion with existing companies exceed the number of opportunities for recruiting new businesses to their communities.

> **Business Retention and Expansion** …focuses on encouraging existing local businesses to remain in the community and/or to expand their operations and workforce.

In addition to the value of becoming more familiar with the current status and growth possibilities of local businesses, retention and expansion efforts typically offer specific business assistance such as business counseling, access to financing, workforce development programs and information on best practices and industry trends.

Communities can employ a variety of approaches to foster the expansion of existing companies. One of these methods is to conduct a Business Retention & Expansion (BR&E) program. A BR&E approach features a systematic outreach to existing companies to identify their needs, challenges and opportunities. Several programs are available that can be adapted for the specific needs of a particular community.

Benefits of the BR&E approach include:

- Identifying opportunities to encourage the expansion of new companies

- Identifying opportunities to avert pending job losses or business closures

- Ability to take a community-wide approach to addressing business needs

- A systematic way to collect information

- Ability to immediately identify solutions for businesses

- Opportunity to engage civic groups or volunteers to partner in the work

- Building good public relations for municipalities and economic development organizations

- Identifying vendor and subcontractor business networking opportunities

By meeting the needs of existing businesses, the stage is also better set for successful business recruitment efforts. Potential new businesses to a new community may investigate the satisfaction of existing businesses, and base a portion of their business location decision on satisfaction levels.

A broad array of factors impacts a community's ability to foster job creation through its existing business base.

First and foremost, a community must have a nucleus of business activity to begin with. The greater the size and diversity of the business base, the more opportunity exists for the creation of jobs with this strategy.

A proactive, working partnership between the business and education communities is also critical for job growth. Communities that develop effective partnerships between businesses and community colleges and/or four-year institutions can create business growth.

The psychological importance of business owners feeling a part of the community—and supported by their local government—also has a positive impact on future job creation.

It is generally agreed that more jobs are created by businesses that are growing at their existing location than by businesses that expand through relocation. Cultivating a fertile environment for local business activity, therefore, can be the most effective strategy for both short- and long-term job creation.

Examples of Strategic Implementation Activities

- Systematic outreach to businesses
- Forums and training sessions
- Business finance workshops
- Workforce development initiatives
- Promotion of business incentives
- Streamlining local government regulations

Advantages	Drawbacks
• Identifying opportunities to encourage the expansion of new companies • Identifying opportunities to avert pending job losses or business closures • Ability to take a community-wide approach to addressing business needs • A systematic way to collect information • Ability to immediately identify solutions for businesses • Opportunity to engage civic groups or volunteers to partner in the work • Building good public relations for municipalities and economic development organizations • Identifying vendor and sub-contractor business networking opportunities	• Potential for significant effort that only gains marginal and dispersed benefit

Key Success Factors

- Ability to compete in a global market
- Access to small-business financing
- Availability of local buildings
- Availability of local infrastructure
- Availability of local land
- Capable, experienced economic development professionals
- Local, available, high-skill labor pool
- Local, available, low-skill labor pool
- Local pro-business climate
- Strong relations between economic development organization and local businesses
- Sufficient base of local businesses
- Support from local education professionals at all levels

Business Cultivation

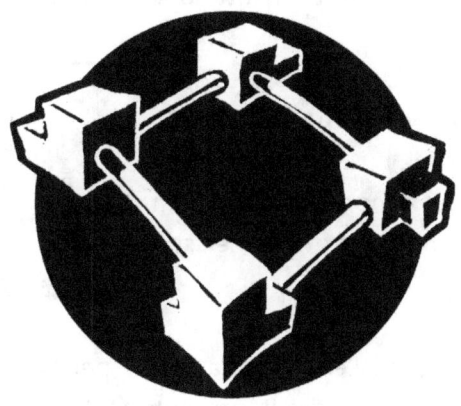

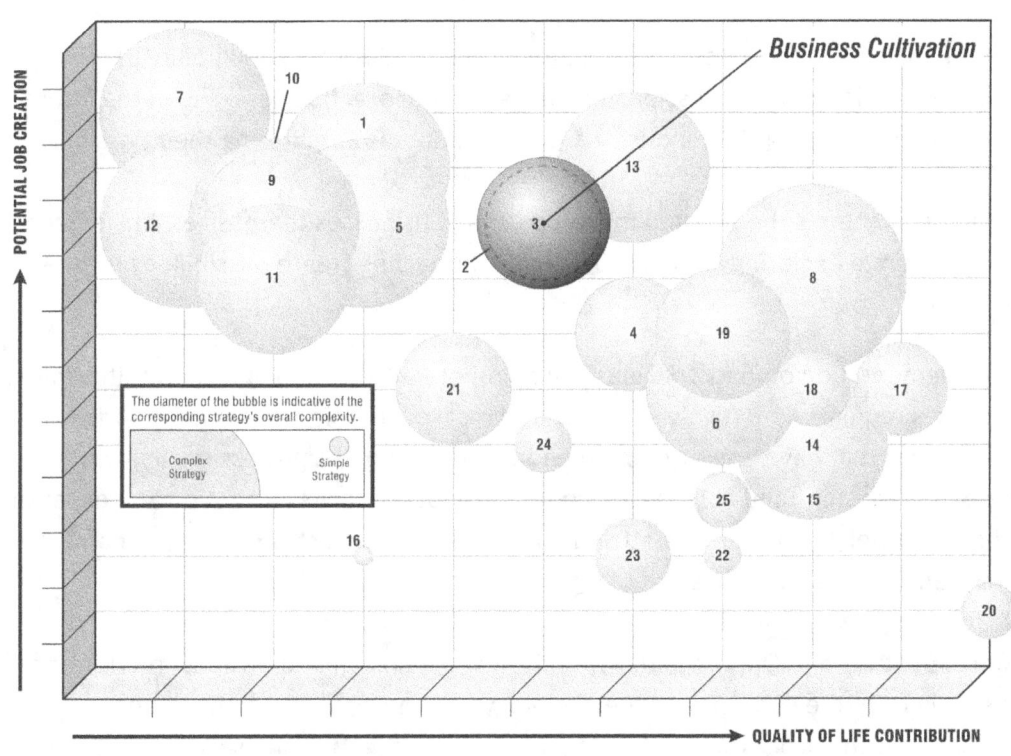

The diameter of the bubble is indicative of the corresponding strategy's overall complexity.

Complex Strategy

Simple Strategy

POTENTIAL JOB CREATION

QUALITY OF LIFE CONTRIBUTION

Business Cultivation

1. Business Recruitment
2. Business Retention & Expansion
3. Business Cultivation
4. Entrepreneurial Development
5. Energy Development
6. Environmental Restoration
7. Logistics Centers
8. Leading-edge Development
9. Value-added Agriculture
10. Value-added Forest Products
11. Value-added Fisheries
12. Value-added Mining
13. Destination Tourism
14. Cultural Tourism
15. Local/Regional Tourism
16. Pass-through Visitor Services
17. Downtown Development
18. Education Development
19. Health Care Expansion
20. Bedroom Community Development
21. Infrastructure Development
22. Attracting Retirees
23. Attracting Lone Eagles
24. Attracting Government Jobs
25. Attracting Funding

Business Cultivation

Business Cultivation is a new term used to describe as many as three economic development methodologies: import substitution, industrial clusters and WealthWorks.

In effect, Business Cultivation is "Business Retention and Expansion version 2.0." While the ultimate objective—supporting existing businesses—is the same, Business Cultivation is a more specific and in-depth approach to facilitating the growth of existing businesses.

> **Business Cultivation**
> ...includes as many as three targeted approaches to expand and/or retain existing businesses. This is a more in-depth and sophisticated approach to business retention and expansion.

The ability to understand the local economy, and the specific dynamics of the businesses and industries that comprise it, presents a job-creating opportunity for many communities.

Most important to the success of this strategy is the willingness and ability of the local economic development professionals to engage with local businesses with the intent of not only understanding their industry and needs, but also organizing their possibilities.

Another key factor is the size and make-up of the businesses themselves. Businesses that are open to exploring new collaborative approaches create possibilities for the community.

The implementation of industrial clustering, import substitution and/or WealthWorks techniques requires a relatively sophisticated local economic development office. Communities that have one or more economic development professional(s) with the tenure, relationships and abilities may be able to take business retention and expansion to the next level. Without these attributes, however, such a strategy may become no more than a fruitless exercise.

Import Substitution. Opportunities for business expansion and business recruitment can evolve from the concept and methodology of import substitution. Import substitution is the process of identifying raw materials, goods and services that are "imported" into the city/county/region that have the potential to be produced and provided locally.

One example is the provision of cabinetry for the recreational vehicle industry. If a community has one or more recreational vehicle manufacturers that are purchasing cabinetry out of the county/region in large quantities, there may be a business case for an existing or new local company to fabricate and provide the cabinetry. Many other examples exist in other industries and sectors. As such, based on identifying products and services imported into an area in at least modest volumes, business development strategies can be created.

Industrial Clusters. Similarly, communities may wish to convene representatives of industrial clusters—businesses and/or suppliers in the same economic sector—to explore mutual and/or complementary opportunities for growth. This concept was introduced and popularized by Michael Porter in his 1990 book, *The Competitive Advantage of Nations*. Porter claims that clusters have the potential to affect competition in three ways: by increasing the productivity of the companies in the cluster, by driving innovation and by stimulating new businesses in the field.

By bringing together the cluster of businesses within an industry, many opportunities and benefits present themselves for communities. These include:

- Efficiencies can be gained by understanding and advancing the needs of an entire industry rather than simply one business at a time.

- Frequently new business relationships between and among individuals in the same community generate advantages simply by getting to know one another.

- Communities can "adopt an issue." That is, a group of business leaders can identify a problem or issue that can best be addressed and advanced by local government or economic development organizations. Goodwill is built and jobs can be retained or created.

- Import substitution opportunities can be realized. A group of similar businesses may be able to identify new business opportunities (suppliers, professional services, etc.) that may generate business activity and create jobs by producing locally what has been "imported" into the city/ county/region.

WealthWorks. WealthWorks is an approach to community and economic development that utilizes a broad definition of "wealth" to guide increasing such wealth through first identifying specific market opportunities and then constructing "value chains" to create and gauge their wealth-building impact.

The eight forms of wealth include individual, intellectual, social, cultural, natural, built, political and financial capital. From this broader construct of capital/wealth, a market opportunity is identified and documented that—with the right set of investments and connections—could generate wealth-building results. Market opportunities can be identified in any number of sectors such as agriculture, forest products and energy.

The next step is designed to connect the various forms of capital to a specific market opportunity. This is done by creating a WealthWorks value chain. This value chain is a coordinated network of people, businesses, organizations and agencies that can address a market opportunity to meet demand for specific products or services. The entire effort must be orchestrated by a coordinator, which can be a local organization, agency or team of interested partners and/or businesses. Value chains are then developed to address gaps, bottlenecks or under-utilized resources in order to generate wealth.

Examples of Strategic Implementation Activities

- Researching local businesses for import substitution opportunities
- Convening business cluster roundtables
- Initiate a WealthWorks-based project

Advantages	Drawbacks
• Efficiencies can be gained by understanding and advancing the needs of an entire industry rather than simply one business at a time • Frequently new business relationships between individuals in the same community generate advantages simply by getting to know one another • Communities can "adopt an issue." That is, a group of business leaders can identify a problem or issue that can best be addressed and advanced by local government or economic development organizations. Goodwill is built, and jobs can be retained or created • Creation of goodwill by supporting local businesses • Reinforces the value of the local economic development organization in the eyes of businesses and the community at-large • Import substitution opportunities can be realized. A group of similar businesses may be able to identify new business opportunities (suppliers, professional services, etc.) that may generate business activity and create jobs by producing locally what has been "imported" into the city/county/region	• Potential for significant effort that only gains marginal and dispersed benefit

Key Success Factors

- Ability to identify product and service gaps
- Access to small-business financing
- Availability of local buildings
- Availability of local infrastructure
- Availability of local land
- Capable, experienced economic development professionals
- Local, available, high-skill labor pool
- Local, available, low-skill labor pool
- Local pro-business climate
- Proximity and access to markets
- Strong relations between economic development organization and local businesses
- Sufficient base of local businesses

Entrepreneurial Development

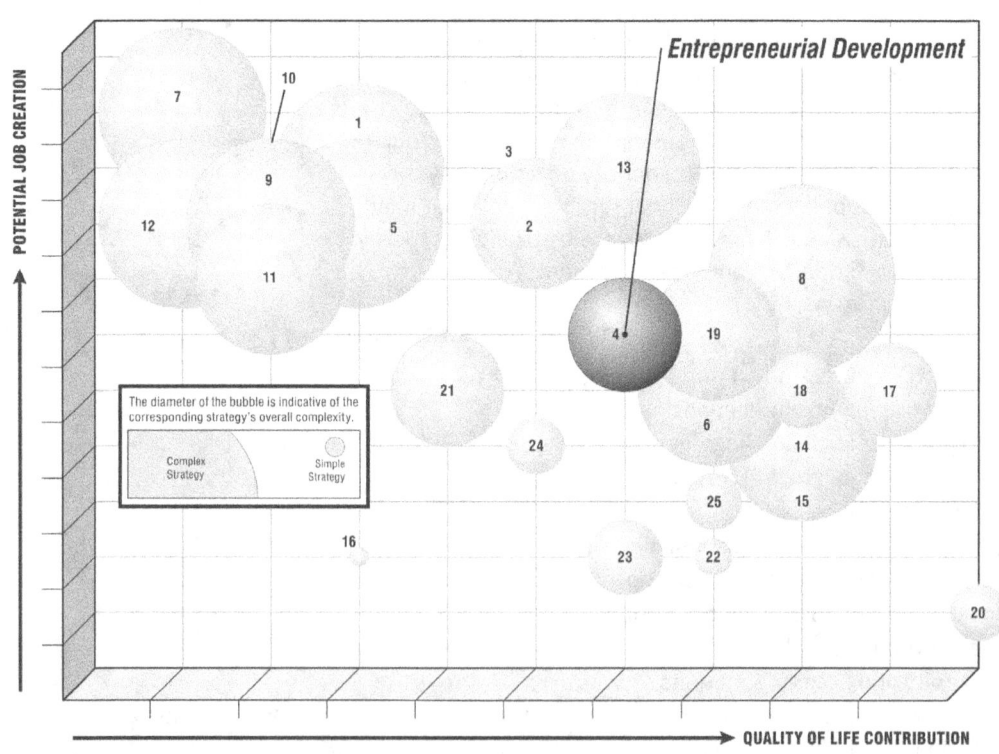

1. Business Recruitment
2. Business Retention & Expansion
3. Business Cultivation
4. Entrepreneurial Development
5. Energy Development
6. Environmental Restoration
7. Logistics Centers
8. Leading-edge Development
9. Value-added Agriculture
10. Value-added Forest Products
11. Value-added Fisheries
12. Value-added Mining
13. Destination Tourism
14. Cultural Tourism
15. Local/Regional Tourism
16. Pass-through Visitor Services
17. Downtown Development
18. Education Development
19. Health Care Expansion
20. Bedroom Community Development
21. Infrastructure Development
22. Attracting Retirees
23. Attracting Lone Eagles
24. Attracting Government Jobs
25. Attracting Funding

Entrepreneurial Development

Small businesses represent over 99% of all employers in the United States. People establish businesses based upon unique skills, passion and a perceived market opportunity.

Frequently missing in a community-based economic development strategy is a concerted approach to facilitating the start-up and growth of entrepreneurial ventures.

> **Entrepreneurial Development**
> ...is a set of activities designed to encourage and support aspiring and existing entrepreneurs to establish and/or further develop their businesses.

Also referred to as microenterprise development, communities may offer programming to assist businesses with access to capital, resources for workforce training, business coaching and/or partnerships with local educational institutions.

Entrepreneurial Development approaches are becoming increasingly sophisticated. More recently referred to as *economic gardening,* some communities now provide such resources as expertise for search engine optimization, information about new business models and ways to better use social media.

Key to capturing the entrepreneurial job-creating potential of any community is an orchestrated effort led by an individual trained in business coaching and support. A systematic approach to reach current and aspiring entrepreneurs to encourage them, and then to provide access to business development resources (business planning, small business finance, etc.), can foster entrepreneurship within a community.

Communities that have a sufficient base of such entrepreneurial activity have definite potential for business start-ups and spin-offs of existing businesses.

While creating jobs by capturing the entrepreneurial potential of a community holds promise for many communities, the dispersed nature of successful start-ups often makes it difficult for the community to see the benefit. Unlike one company that might employ 20 or more individuals, entrepreneurial start-ups frequently begin with just one or two jobs.

Other than the time and resources invested by professionals and volunteers, there is very little cost or downside to the Entrepreneurial Development strategy. Every community likes to believe that they are fostering a pro-business environment for all of their residents.

Examples of Strategic Implementation Activities
• Establishment of business coaching position • Establishment of local business advisory board • Establishment of micro-enterprise loan fund • Providing forums promoting entrepreneurship

Advantages	Drawbacks
• Cultivating community potential • Building goodwill within business community and community-at-large	• Very dispersed job creation (frequently not noticeable) • High risk of business failures

Key Success Factors
• Access to small-business financing • Dedicated business coaching staff • High-speed Internet • Local pro-business climate • Sufficient local entrepreneurial base • Supportive post-secondary education and training programs

Energy Development

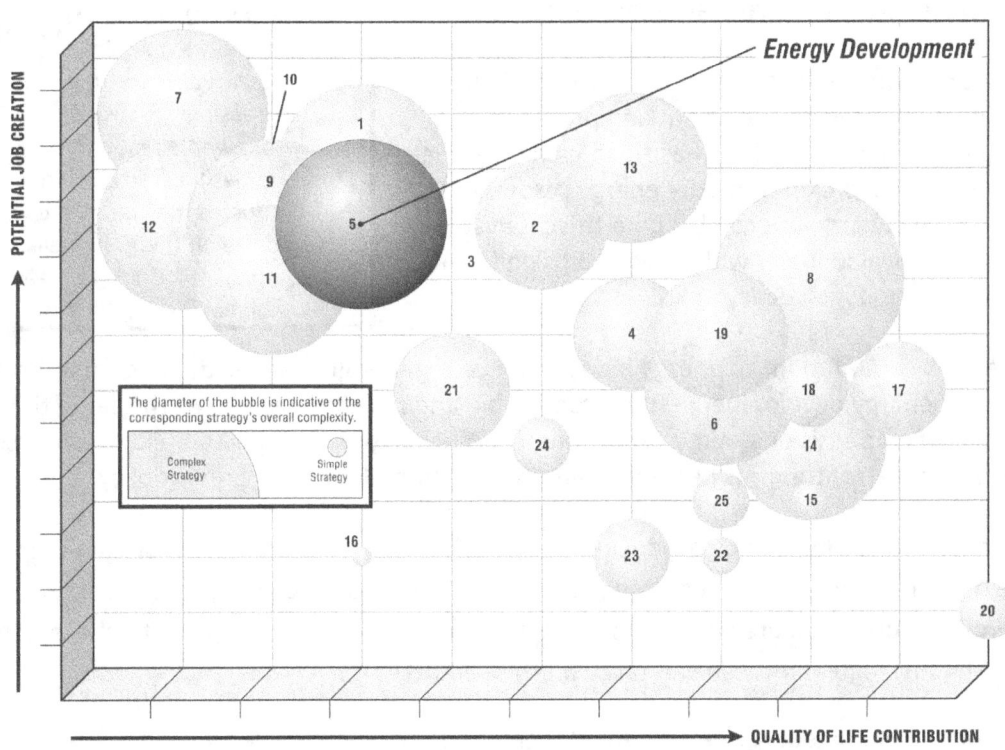

The diameter of the bubble is indicative of the corresponding strategy's overall complexity.

Complex Strategy — Simple Strategy

POTENTIAL JOB CREATION

QUALITY OF LIFE CONTRIBUTION

Energy Development

1. Business Recruitment
2. Business Retention & Expansion
3. Business Cultivation
4. Entrepreneurial Development
5. Energy Development
6. Environmental Restoration
7. Logistics Centers
8. Leading-edge Development
9. Value-added Agriculture
10. Value-added Forest Products
11. Value-added Fisheries
12. Value-added Mining
13. Destination Tourism
14. Cultural Tourism
15. Local/Regional Tourism
16. Pass-through Visitor Services
17. Downtown Development
18. Education Development
19. Health Care Expansion
20. Bedroom Community Development
21. Infrastructure Development
22. Attracting Retirees
23. Attracting Lone Eagles
24. Attracting Government Jobs
25. Attracting Funding

Energy Development

Energy development has been one of the fastest growing industries and effective economic development strategies for job creation throughout the early part of the 21st Century. Public policy has largely focused upon providing support to the renewable energy sector, while traditional forms of energy development such as oil and gas have been exceptionally strong economically during the period of 2009-2014.

Many of the fastest growing U.S. states with the strongest economies over the past six years have experienced economic growth due to advancements in the energy sector.

Renewable energy options include wind, solar, biomass, bio-energy, geothermal, nuclear and hydropower.

Both the federal government and many states have approved new policies and incentives to foster the development of the renewable energy industry.

While larger, established companies may have an edge in capitalizing on many of these business opportunities, viable start-up options exist based upon proximity to renewable energy supplies and local market demand.

For many states and communities, traditional non-renewable energy development and production using coal, oil or natural gas has significant potential. In these cases, proximity to the energy resource is not only necessary, but can become the catalyst in creating a local industry with or without significant local community advocacy.

> **Energy Development**
> ...is rapidly expanding in an industrial sector that is increasingly focusing on renewable resources. Communities located close to such resources may be able to capitalize on them, as well as traditional resources to create higher-paying jobs.

America's commitment to energy independence is generally seen as dependent upon all forms of energy development—both renewable and non-renewable. At the same time, increasing emphasis on energy conservation—efficiency though green building practices and energy retrofitting—is becoming a more common element in public policy.

The ability to create jobs by producing energy is heavily dependent upon proximity to one or more energy resources. Communities that can attract companies with access to energy resources, secure power-purchase agreements, and can comply with challenging government regulations can capitalize on this sector.

Without question, energy development is the sector of the past decade—if not the coming century. The ability of nations to produce energy while meeting environmental goals is dominating political and economic decision making.

While economic downturns may temporarily relieve pressure to develop energy resources, in the long-term, the energy development sector will continue to experience strong growth.

Examples of Strategic Implementation Activities
• Attraction of energy development firms to capitalize on the availability of energy resources • Pursuit of a community-based renewable energy project (wind farm, for example) • Advocacy for improvement to energy infrastructure (transmission line, for example) • Establishment of local renewable energy zones (tax advantages for businesses)

Advantages	Drawbacks
• Likely to be a fast-growth industry for the foreseeable future • Positive governmental tax-base implications • Opportunity for rural communities	• Potential local opposition to some forms of energy development

Key Success Factors
• Ability to build a team of energy-development experts • Ability to secure power-purchase agreements • Access to large-scale capital • Availability of energy resources • Capable, experienced economic development professionals • Local government support • Proximity to transmission lines with excess capacity • Supportive state energy policies and incentives

Environmental Restoration

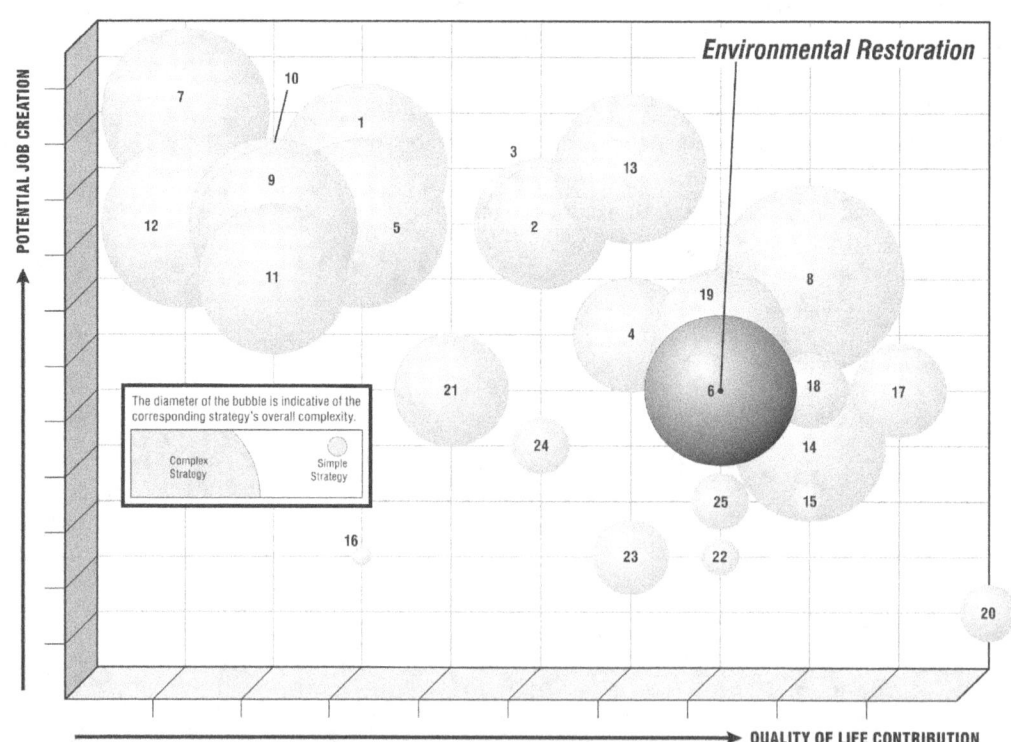

1. Business Recruitment	7. Logistics Centers	13. Destination Tourism	19. Health Care Expansion
2. Business Retention & Expansion	8. Leading-edge Development	14. Cultural Tourism	20. Bedroom Community Development
3. Business Cultivation	9. Value-added Agriculture	15. Local/Regional Tourism	21. Infrastructure Development
4. Entrepreneurial Development	10. Value-added Forest Products	16. Pass-through Visitor Services	22. Attracting Retirees
5. Energy Development	11. Value-added Fisheries	17. Downtown Development	23. Attracting Lone Eagles
6. Environmental Restoration	12. Value-added Mining	18. Education Development	24. Attracting Government Jobs
			25. Attracting Funding

Environmental Restoration

Communities have the opportunity to "turn lemons into lemonade" by focusing on derelict industrial buildings and sites for redevelopment.

Frequently, communities may have old industrial sites not currently in use. These sites may relate to natural resource-based extraction industries that may have utilized chemicals or compounds that have left the industrial land unusable for future use without first completing clean-up activities.

> **Environmental Restoration**
> ...presents the opportunity to create jobs and enhance quality of life by reclaiming land from Brownfield and other sites such as closed military bases and gasoline stations for industrial and business parks, improving forest health and increasing potable water supplies.

The benefits of this strategy are twofold: 1) jobs can be created initially by clean-up activities; and 2) the former industrial site becomes available for promotion and development, thus creating jobs in the longer-term.

First and foremost, communities must have an eligible site(s) for an Environmental Restoration strategy. One or more former industrial sites that have environmental contamination preventing future redevelopment are essential to advance this strategy. These sites are frequently referred to as Brownfield sites.

A community must then mobilize itself by first assessing the condition of the property, and then developing a specific action plan to remediate the environmental problem.

Of critical importance is the formation of a local team that can network with state and/or federal contacts to attract the funding necessary to assess and address the environmental problem. Communities must then have the local sophistication to redevelop and market the restored site for future use.

Communities may find the restoration of contaminated industrial sites to be a much greater challenge than the establishment of a Greenfield (one without environmental contamination) industrial site. As such, the availability of existing or prospective Greenfield industrial site development becomes a factor in the importance and relative urgency of this strategy.

Additionally, communities that are pursuing a business recruitment and/or business retention/expansion strategy may find this Environmental Restoration strategy to be relatively more important.

Finally, an Environmental Restoration strategy can entail more than simply the redevelopment of industrial sites. Communities that are proximate to forests, for example, may implement this strategy to restore the environmental health of forests while creating by-products valuable to either a value-added wood products strategy and/or an energy development (biomass) strategy. This strategy is also relevant to communities considering reusing former military bases and depots.

Examples of Strategic Implementation Activities
• Completing an environmental review or environmental impact statement on one or more parcels of affected land • Seeking government funding for environmental studies and/or land remediation • Creating jobs through remediating affected industrial lands • Military base clean-up and reuse

Advantages	Drawbacks
• Improving the environment and remediating a "community eyesore" • Potential to attract governmental funding • Long-term location for job creation	• Time-intensive and expensive upfront costs • Economic benefits are typically only long-term

Key Success Factors
• Access to large-scale capital • Availability of Brownfield sites • Capable, experienced economic development professionals • Local government support • Strong state and/or federal legislative delegation(s)

Logistics Centers

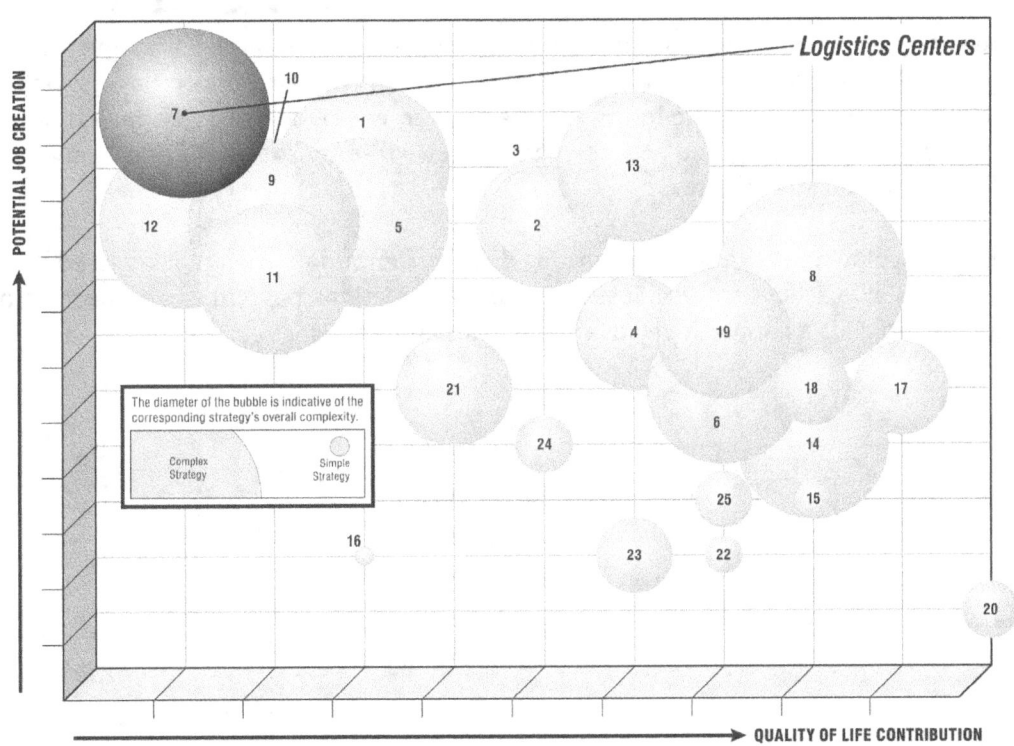

The diameter of the bubble is indicative of the corresponding strategy's overall complexity.

Complex Strategy

Simple Strategy

POTENTIAL JOB CREATION

QUALITY OF LIFE CONTRIBUTION

Logistics Centers

1. Business Recruitment
2. Business Retention & Expansion
3. Business Cultivation
4. Entrepreneurial Development
5. Energy Development
6. Environmental Restoration

7. Logistics Centers
8. Leading-edge Development
9. Value-added Agriculture
10. Value-added Forest Products
11. Value-added Fisheries
12. Value-added Mining

13. Destination Tourism
14. Cultural Tourism
15. Local/Regional Tourism
16. Pass-through Visitor Services
17. Downtown Development
18. Education Development

19. Health Care Expansion
20. Bedroom Community Development
21. Infrastructure Development
22. Attracting Retirees
23. Attracting Lone Eagles
24. Attracting Government Jobs
25. Attracting Funding

Logistics Centers

As larger corporations continue to grow and increasingly dominate business, many of them need to locate large-scale logistics and distribution centers in strategic locations throughout the nation.

These companies take a very calculated, strategic approach to siting such facilities. Several factors can significantly influence these siting decisions, including proximity to their network of stores/outlets, proximity to the interstate highway system and sometimes proximity to rail service and ports.

For communities located along these strategic transportation corridors and facilities, recruiting logistics centers can have very large payoffs.

> **Logistics Centers**
> ...are needed by mid-size to large companies as a cost-effective means for managing and transporting goods/other resources from production sites for further processing, or to sales outlets. Communities with suitable transportation infrastructure and location advantages may capitalize on this strategy to create a large number of jobs.

To be successful with such recruiting, communities must be prepared with large tracts of industrial land with superior access to one or more of these transportation assets, and have appropriate available infrastructure (power, water, sewer, etc.). In addition, they should be well connected with relevant industry trade associations and regularly attend their annual trade shows.

Business development site selectors often advise corporations when making large investments in logistics centers. Fostering business relationships with such site selectors therefore provides a competitive advantage in pursuing logistics centers.

Examples of Strategic Implementation Activities

- Development of industrial land base
- Recruiting distribution centers through attending logistics tradeshows
- Identification of targeted businesses seeking logistics centers within the region

Advantages	Drawbacks
• Large-scale job creation	• Potential for traffic congestion • Generally below-average wages

Key Success Factors

- Ability to network and attend relevant trade shows
- Availability of industrially zoned land for industrial park development
- Availability of local buildings
- Availability of local infrastructure
- Availability of local land
- Capable, experienced economic development professionals
- Competitive recruitment incentives
- Local, available, high-skill labor pool
- Local, available, low-skill labor pool
- Local government support
- Relationship with site selectors
- Strategic location for logistics center

Leading-edge Development

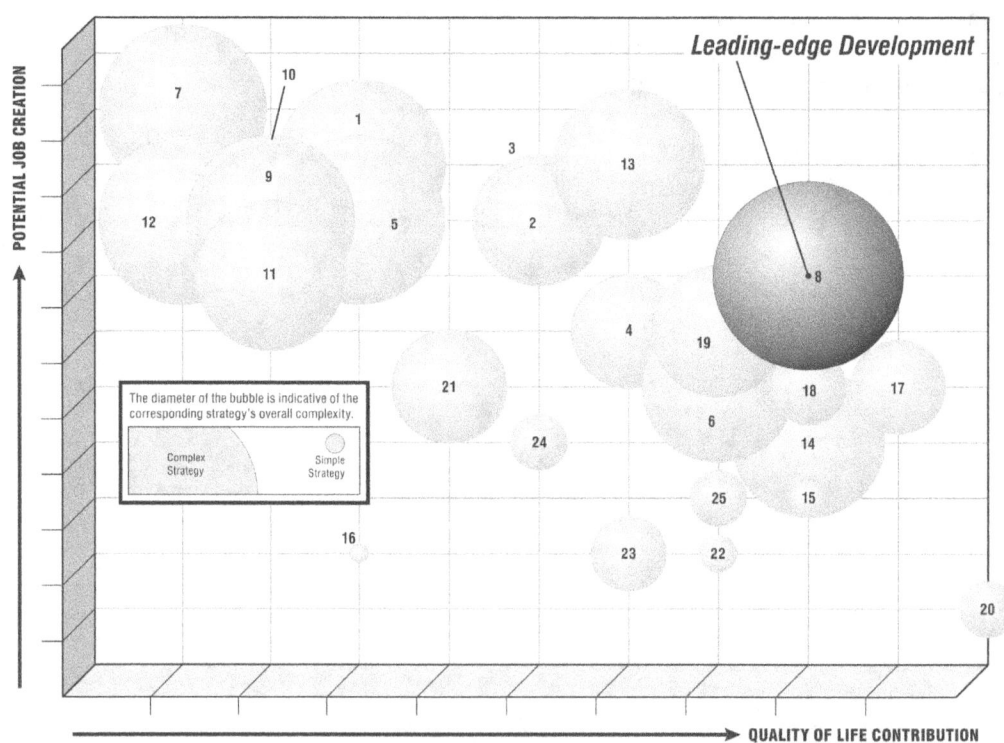

The diameter of the bubble is indicative of the corresponding strategy's overall complexity.

Complex Strategy   Simple Strategy

POTENTIAL JOB CREATION

QUALITY OF LIFE CONTRIBUTION

Leading-edge Development

1. Business Recruitment
2. Business Retention & Expansion
3. Business Cultivation
4. Entrepreneurial Development
5. Energy Development
6. Environmental Restoration
7. Logistics Centers
8. Leading-edge Development
9. Value-added Agriculture
10. Value-added Forest Products
11. Value-added Fisheries
12. Value-added Mining
13. Destination Tourism
14. Cultural Tourism
15. Local/Regional Tourism
16. Pass-through Visitor Services
17. Downtown Development
18. Education Development
19. Health Care Expansion
20. Bedroom Community Development
21. Infrastructure Development
22. Attracting Retirees
23. Attracting Lone Eagles
24. Attracting Government Jobs
25. Attracting Funding

Leading-edge Development

Virtually since the invention of the wheel, mankind has developed business applications for new inventions. From the cotton gin, to the automobile, to the telephone and to the steam engine, leading-edge thinking has transformed America and established the nation as a world leader in business and economics.

> **Leading-edge Development**
> ...is a strategy that harnesses the intellectual and creative capacity of a community to research and develop ideas into products, especially in new technologies, including, e.g., information processing, energy and bio-sciences.

For communities, this creates an opportunity for economic development. Fostering and harnessing the creative and intellectual capacity of its citizenry can generate new and expanded businesses, creating high-wage jobs.

Of the 25 strategies, however, Leading-edge Development is the most complex strategy to implement. Communities must have extraordinary competitive advantages with respect to the intellectual and creative capacity of its citizenry, and organizations such as higher education institutions must be available and focused in order to cultivate such opportunities.

Leading-edge Development comes with many different titles, depending upon the regions and institutions advancing similar efforts. This strategy is often referred to as technology-led development, entrepreneurial development, and high tech, among other monikers. Here we use the name Leading-edge Development to describe efforts that typically:

- Focus on the application of technology (although not exclusively)

- Require sophisticated management teams

- Need the transfer of technology from educational institutions

- Need angel investors or venture capital

- Have national and/or international markets

Leading-edge Development is distinguished from Entrepreneurial Development and Business Cultivation generally by the level of sophistication of the product or service, and distinguished from Business Recruitment by the specificity of focus on one application.

Perhaps the most important factor for communities is their proximity and relationship with a nearby higher educational institution. Colleges and universities often have research and development as a part of their mission, and relationships with communities can be win/win.

Examples of Strategic Implementation Activities

- Business management, coaching and advising
- Business incubation program
- Mentoring program, including free services from area professionals (law, accounting, marketing, financing including venture capital, patent advisement and more)
- Introductions to angel investors
- Collaboration with university research teams
- Networking and educational events
- Lunch seminars

Advantages	Drawbacks
- High-wage job creation - Creation of positive business climate and reputation - Creation of industry clusters - Fostering an entrepreneurial environment	- Highly demanding of experts' time - Capital costs for buildings and programs

Key Success Factors

- Ability to compete in a global market
- Access to large-scale capital
- Adequate telecommunications infrastructure
- Availability of local buildings
- Availability of local infrastructure
- Availability of local land
- Availability of urban services
- Capable, experienced economic development professionals
- Collaboration of economic development staff and educational community
- Competitive recruitment incentives
- Dedicated local financial resources for staffing recruiters
- Local, available, high-skill labor pool
- Local, available, low-skill labor pool
- Local government support
- Proximity and access to markets
- Proximity to scheduled air service
- Sufficient local entrepreneurial base
- Supportive post-secondary education and training programs

Value-added Agriculture

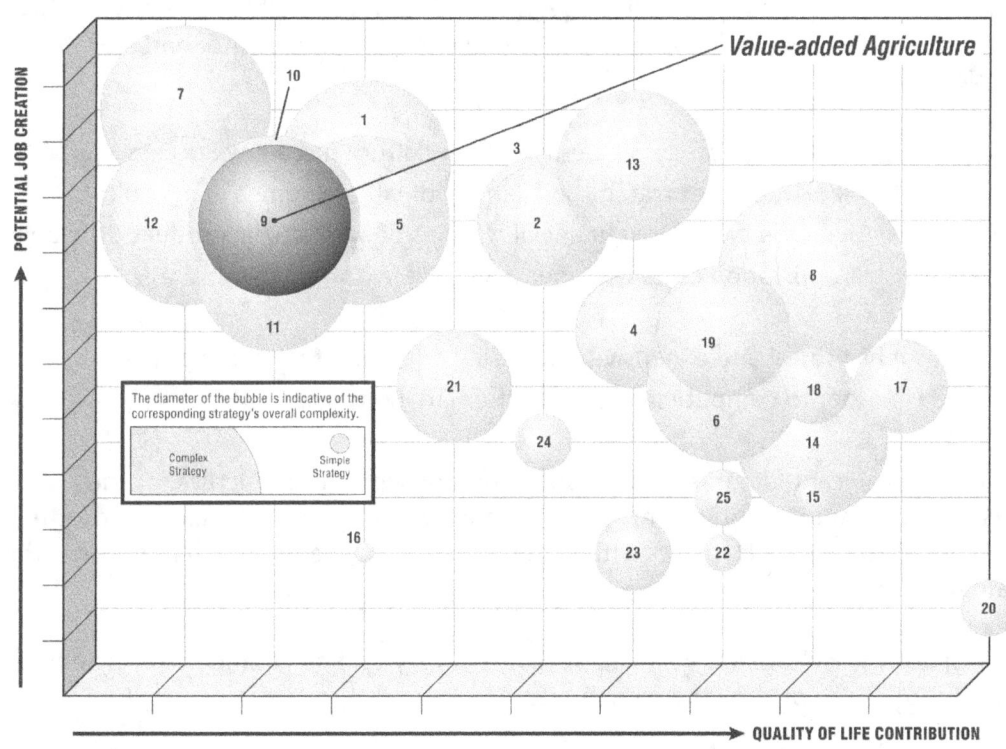

Value-added Agriculture

POTENTIAL JOB CREATION

The diameter of the bubble is indicative of the corresponding strategy's overall complexity.

Complex Strategy

Simple Strategy

QUALITY OF LIFE CONTRIBUTION

1. Business Recruitment
2. Business Retention & Expansion
3. Business Cultivation
4. Entrepreneurial Development
5. Energy Development
6. Environmental Restoration
7. Logistics Centers
8. Leading-edge Development
9. Value-added Agriculture
10. Value-added Forest Products
11. Value-added Fisheries
12. Value-added Mining
13. Destination Tourism
14. Cultural Tourism
15. Local/Regional Tourism
16. Pass-through Visitor Services
17. Downtown Development
18. Education Development
19. Health Care Expansion
20. Bedroom Community Development
21. Infrastructure Development
22. Attracting Retirees
23. Attracting Lone Eagles
24. Attracting Government Jobs
25. Attracting Funding

Value-added Agriculture

Counties—and frequently clusters of counties—may produce an inordinate amount of one or more agricultural products based upon competitive advantages such as soil types, climate and elevation.

If sufficient volumes of individual raw materials are produced, communities may have an opportunity to "add value" to the commodities through processing. Examples include producing French fries from potatoes, sugar from sugar beets/sugar cane, steaks from cattle and wine from grapes.

Advantages from value-added agricultural business include retaining profits and job-creation opportunities locally, providing jobs consistent with skill levels of the local labor force and reinforcing the culture and economy of local communities.

> **Value-added Agriculture**
> ...is the establishment or expansion of area businesses that add value to raw agricultural commodities before they are purchased locally or exported. Producing and selling sugar from sugar cane and French fries from potatoes are examples.

Drawbacks from a Value-added Agriculture strategy typically include a high demand on local utilities (typically water, sewer and power), frequently below-to-average wage levels and sometimes undesirable wastewater and air emissions.

Perhaps as much as any strategy, Value-added Agriculture has a Key Success Factor that dominates the viability of the strategy: availability of large volumes of agricultural commodities. Given the typical low financial margins of agricultural products, the ability to overcome transportation costs becomes a limiting factor for this strategy.

Similarly, sophisticated and expensive processing equipment must typically be purchased in order to compete in the agricultural marketplace.

One other significant factor is the availability of municipal infrastructure for the processing or manufacturing plant. Communities without the availability—and/or the willingness—to serve such plants with water and sewer systems should not pursue this strategy.

Value-added Agriculture is a very site-specific strategy that can immediately be either "ruled in" or "ruled out" by the community.

Communities that desire to "rule it in" definitely need to consider some of the possible long-term consequences of the strategy before proceeding.

While a Value-added Agricultural strategy can create a high volume of jobs, additional factors to be weighed before advancing this strategy include the average wage level for the jobs, availability of a benefit package for workers, demands on local infrastructure, demands on transportation infrastructure and any externalities (e.g., water contamination) associated with food processing.

Examples of Strategic Implementation Activities
• Recruitment of large-scale food processing plant • Facilitation of local food product businesses in residential or commercial areas • Establishment of a farmers' market

Advantages	Drawbacks
• Retention of profits and job-creation opportunities locally • Creation of jobs consistent with skill levels of the local labor force • Reinforcement of the culture and economy of local communities	• High demand on local utilities (typically water, sewer, and power) • Below-to-average wage levels • Sometimes undesirable wastewater and air emissions

Key Success Factors
• Ability to successfully market value-added products • Ability to understand industry trends and opportunities • Access to large-scale capital • Availability of local buildings • Availability of local infrastructure • Availability of local land • Excess water and sewer infrastructure capacity • Local, available, high-skill labor pool • Local, available, low-skill labor pool • Proximity and access to markets • Proximity to large volumes of agricultural commodities

Value-added Forest Products

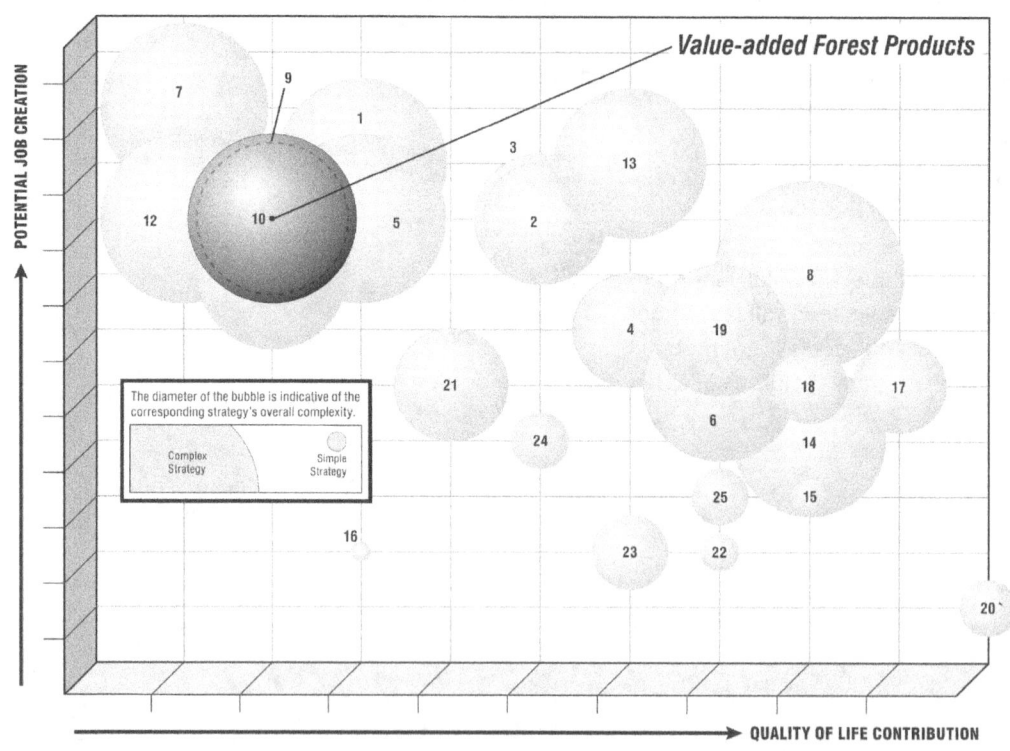

1. Business Recruitment
2. Business Retention & Expansion
3. Business Cultivation
4. Entrepreneurial Development
5. Energy Development
6. Environmental Restoration
7. Logistics Centers
8. Leading-edge Development
9. Value-added Agriculture
10. Value-added Forest Products
11. Value-added Fisheries
12. Value-added Mining
13. Destination Tourism
14. Cultural Tourism
15. Local/Regional Tourism
16. Pass-through Visitor Services
17. Downtown Development
18. Education Development
19. Health Care Expansion
20. Bedroom Community Development
21. Infrastructure Development
22. Attracting Retirees
23. Attracting Lone Eagles
24. Attracting Government Jobs
25. Attracting Funding

Value-added Forest Products

A variety of products can be produced from federal, state and privately owned forests. Most commonly, lumber is produced from timber. Additionally, other products from forests include fuel for biomass energy, hardwood for furniture manufacturing and flooring, mulch for gardening and miscellaneous related items such as mushrooms.

> **Value-added Forest Products**
> ...is a strategy that communities located close to forest lands may pursue. Producing lumber, furniture, pallets and other wood products, especially for export, are examples.

Policy changes on federal forests over the past 20 years have reduced the availability of the timber supply, causing the lumber industry to be more centralized with a few large companies dominating the business. Replacing lost small mill jobs with new jobs in a related industry can be an attractive strategy for communities. At the same time, the nation's increasing demand for renewable energy is increasingly making smaller biomass-to-energy plants economically viable.

Similar to other value-added strategies, the viability of Value-added Forest Products is heavily dependent upon proximity and access to raw materials. Equally important to proximity and access is the long-term contracting authority to purchase and utilize the materials.

The relatively large-scale financial investments in property, plant and equipment that are often needed can be a deterrent for this strategy.

On the plus side, value-added forest product strategies can generate above-average income levels, especially for rural communities.

Over the past two decades, the forest products industry has been impacted by national forest policy and the globalization of the marketplace. While these trends have been generally negative for the industry, emerging world-wide technologies that are in part motivated by environmental considerations may show new promise for value-added forest products.

Recent developments in the forest products industry are worth considering. One example is the development of hybrid poplar plantations in historically non-forested areas for the production of fiber for wood and paper products. This new trend has resulted in growth in this sector for some traditionally non-forest product counties, while communities that have been dependent upon forest product mills for generations are suffering economically.

Examples of Strategic Implementation Activities

- Facilitation of new business activity producing door frames, window molding, furniture and cabinetry
- Collection and processing of secondary forest products
- Collection and transportation of biomass for energy production and other uses

Advantages	Drawbacks
• Reinforces existing community traditions and culture • Higher than average wage jobs • Can contribute to forest sustainability	• Slow- to no-growth industry • Industry subject to political and policy gyrations

Key Success Factors

- Ability to secure long-term contracts for forest materials
- Ability to successfully market value-added products
- Ability to understand industry trends and opportunities
- Access to large-scale capital
- Availability of local buildings
- Availability of local infrastructure
- Availability of local land
- Local, available, high-skill labor pool
- Local, available, low-skill labor pool
- Proximity and access to forests and forest products
- Proximity and access to markets

Value-added Fish Products

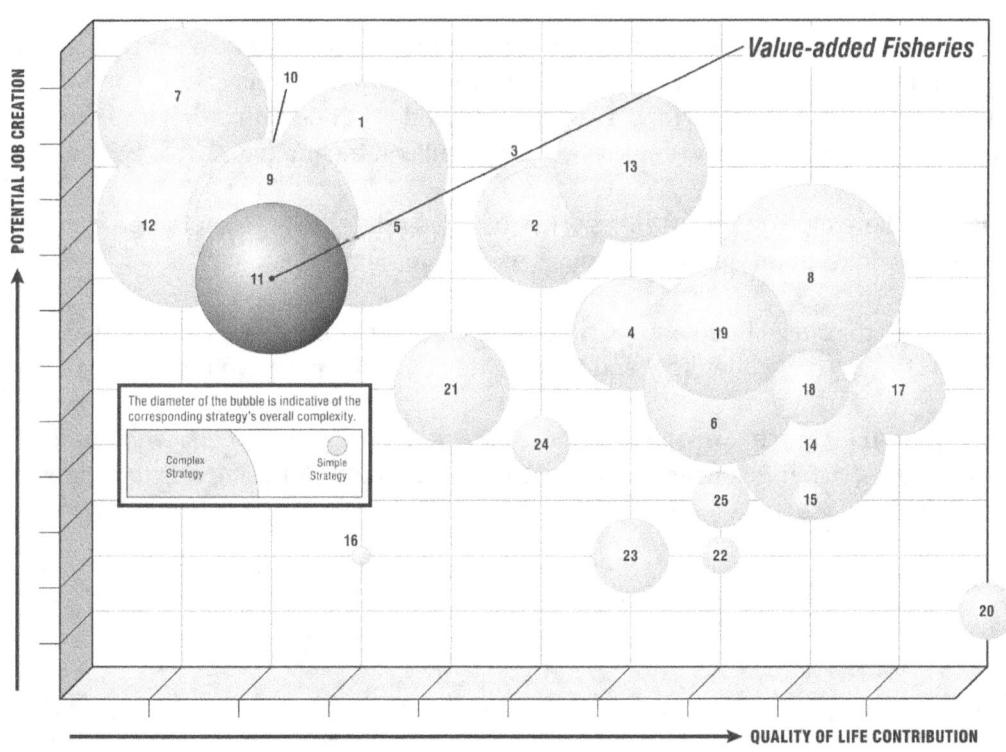

Value-added Fisheries

POTENTIAL JOB CREATION

The diameter of the bubble is indicative of the corresponding strategy's overall complexity.

Complex Strategy   Simple Strategy

QUALITY OF LIFE CONTRIBUTION

1. Business Recruitment
2. Business Retention & Expansion
3. Business Cultivation
4. Entrepreneurial Development
5. Energy Development
6. Environmental Restoration
7. Logistics Centers
8. Leading-edge Development
9. Value-added Agriculture
10. Value-added Forest Products
11. Value-added Fisheries
12. Value-added Mining
13. Destination Tourism
14. Cultural Tourism
15. Local/Regional Tourism
16. Pass-through Visitor Services
17. Downtown Development
18. Education Development
19. Health Care Expansion
20. Bedroom Community Development
21. Infrastructure Development
22. Attracting Retirees
23. Attracting Lone Eagles
24. Attracting Government Jobs
25. Attracting Funding

Value-added Fish Products

Although similar to other natural-resource-based industries that are challenged by availability and volatility of the base commodity, coastal communities have opportunities for adding value to fish products.

Adding value to fish products can mean improvements to the distribution channel to increase the availability of fresh fish, utilization of fish processing by-products such as fertilizer, production of fish oil and altering existing processing methods to increase value.

> **Value-added Fish Products**
> ...is a business development strategy that is especially relevant to fresh and salt water coastal communities. Processing/canning and sale of fish are examples.

The viability of a Value-added Fish Products strategy is dominated by proximity to the fisheries resource. Communities that are close to the ocean, and sometimes to rivers and lakes, may have a unique opportunity to create jobs through various fish processing technologies.

In rare circumstances, a Value-added Fish Products strategy may make sense in inland communities. Aquaculture activities such the production of Tilapia can be conducted in communities far from coastal (and even river) localities. Conditions similar to the natural reproduction of fish are possible using available technology.

Similar to other value-added strategies, key barriers relate to large capital expenditures, including the investment in land, buildings and equipment.

Communities that have been able to break even, or add jobs, with a Value-added Fish Products strategy have been few and far between over the past two decades.

Fluctuations in resource availability and the associated triggering of governmental policies related to harvest have made it extremely difficult for businesses to expand and create jobs in this sector.

Examples of Strategic Implementation Activities

- Fisheries processing, packaging and distribution
- Direct retail outlets
- Maintenance and repair of fisheries equipment

Advantages	Drawbacks
• Job creation • Creation of jobs consistent with existing community traditions and culture	• Slow- to no-growth industry • Industry subject to political and policy gyrations

Key Success Factors

- Ability to understand industry trends and opportunities
- Access to large-scale capital
- Availability of local buildings
- Availability of local infrastructure
- Availability of local land
- Local, available, high-skill labor pool
- Local, available, low-skill labor pool
- Proximity and access to markets
- Proximity to fisheries commodities

Value-added Mining

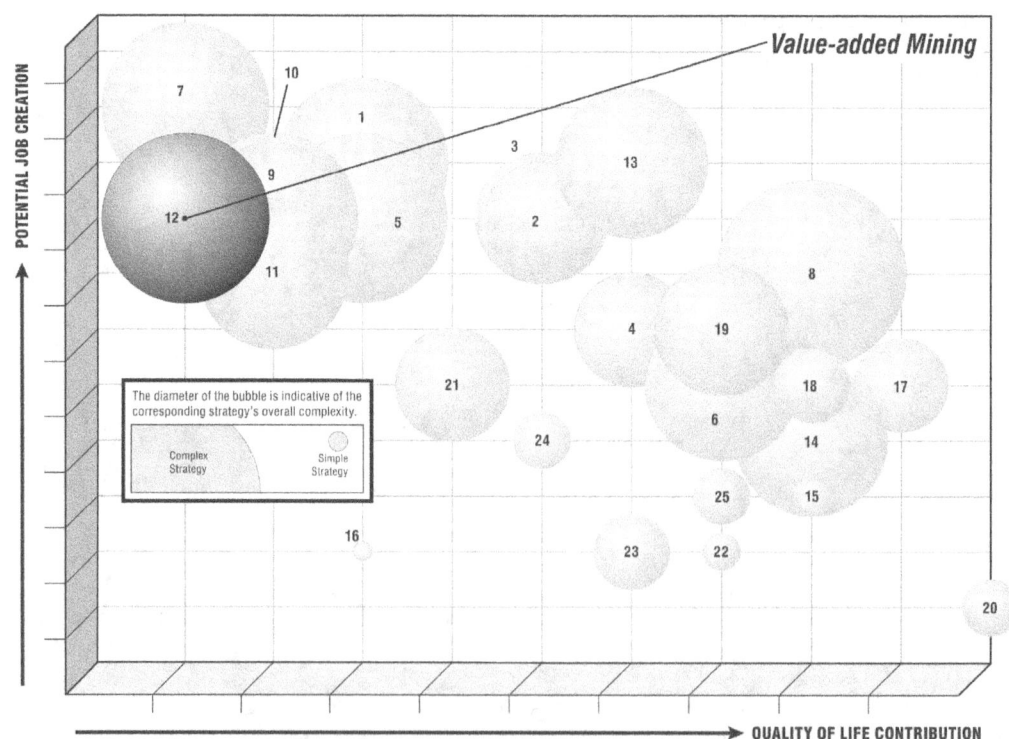

POTENTIAL JOB CREATION

Value-added Mining

The diameter of the bubble is indicative of the corresponding strategy's overall complexity.

Complex Strategy

Simple Strategy

QUALITY OF LIFE CONTRIBUTION

1. Business Recruitment	7. Logistics Centers	13. Destination Tourism
2. Business Retention & Expansion	8. Leading-edge Development	14. Cultural Tourism
3. Business Cultivation	9. Value-added Agriculture	15. Local/Regional Tourism
4. Entrepreneurial Development	10. Value-added Forest Products	16. Pass-through Visitor Services
5. Energy Development	11. Value-added Fisheries	17. Downtown Development
6. Environmental Restoration	12. Value-added Mining	18. Education Development

- 19. Health Care Expansion
- 20. Bedroom Community Development
- 21. Infrastructure Development
- 22. Attracting Retirees
- 23. Attracting Lone Eagles
- 24. Attracting Government Jobs
- 25. Attracting Funding

Value-added Mining

A variety of rock and mineral resources are extracted from the earth for conversion to useful products. Generally, these raw materials become the basis for commercial products through a variety of processes such as crushing, heating and pressure treatment.

For many rural communities, the mining industry has been an economic mainstay for generations. Extraction of minerals such as gold, silver and copper has sustained family wage jobs for decades.

Value-added mineral processing such as steel and aluminum smelting and refining operations are very capital-intensive. A sampling of products include: 1) rolled, cast, forged and extruded products, 2) wire and wire products, 3) nonmetallic mineral products, 4) motor vehicle parts, 5) fabricated metal products and 6) cable for energy and communications firms.

> **Value-added Mining**
> ...presents business development opportunities for communities that have accessible rock and mineral resources that can be processed for sale and export. Production and sale of copper and other metals, as well as pottery from local clay deposits, are examples.

As is the case for the three other value-added strategies, proximity to raw materials is essential for this strategy. Mineral products are usually massive, and therefore generally expensive to transport. As such, the distance between the raw materials and the processing center must be as short as possible. A secondary consideration is the distance from the processing center to the marketplace.

Other key barriers for this strategy include the availability of land, buildings and a suitable labor force.

Global economic forces tend to have a significant impact on this strategy. Trends in commodity prices for gold, silver, platinum and other processed minerals can be a "make-or-break" for this industrial sector.

Political considerations such as state and federal policy related to mineral extraction can also significantly affect the viability of this strategy.

Examples of Strategic Implementation Activities
• Processing of locally or regionally mined minerals
• Support for—and recruitment of—businesses that support the mining industry

Advantages	Drawbacks
• Higher than average wages	• Slow- to no-growth industry • Industry subject to political and policy gyrations

Key Success Factors

- Ability to understand industry trends and opportunities
- Access to large-scale capital
- Availability of local buildings
- Availability of local infrastructure
- Availability of local land
- Local, available, high-skill labor pool
- Local, available, low-skill labor pool
- Proximity and access to markets
- Proximity to raw materials and minerals

Destination Tourism

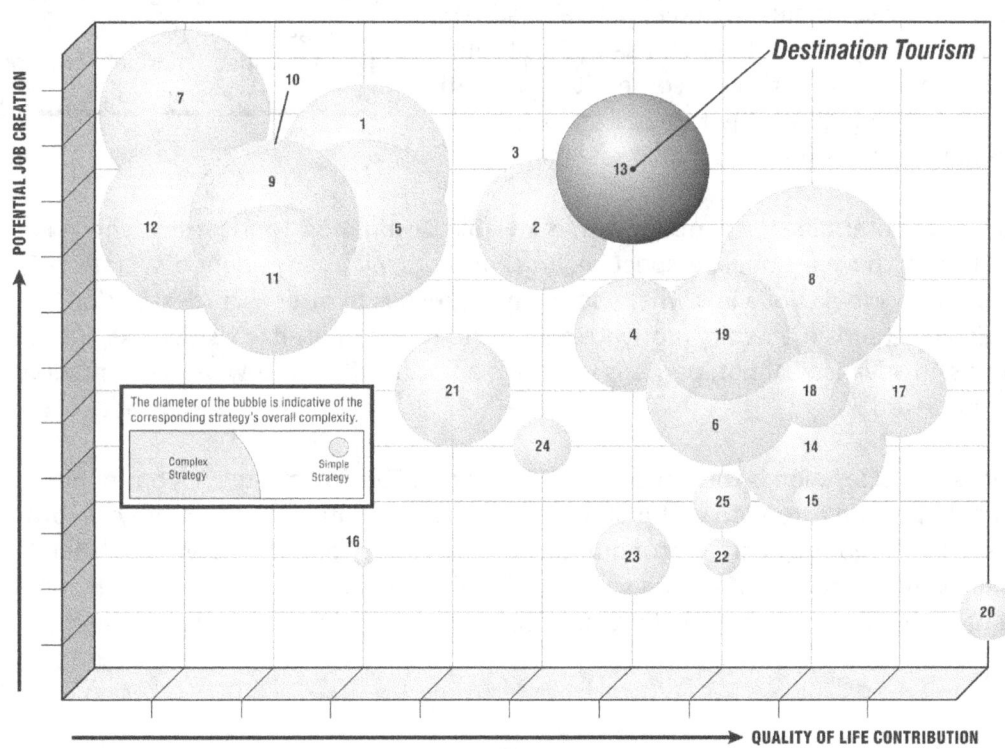

Destination Tourism

POTENTIAL JOB CREATION

The diameter of the bubble is indicative of the corresponding strategy's overall complexity.

Complex Strategy   Simple Strategy

QUALITY OF LIFE CONTRIBUTION

1. Business Recruitment
2. Business Retention & Expansion
3. Business Cultivation
4. Entrepreneurial Development
5. Energy Development
6. Environmental Restoration
7. Logistics Centers
8. Leading-edge Development
9. Value-added Agriculture
10. Value-added Forest Products
11. Value-added Fisheries
12. Value-added Mining
13. Destination Tourism
14. Cultural Tourism
15. Local/Regional Tourism
16. Pass-through Visitor Services
17. Downtown Development
18. Education Development
19. Health Care Expansion
20. Bedroom Community Development
21. Infrastructure Development
22. Attracting Retirees
23. Attracting Lone Eagles
24. Attracting Government Jobs
25. Attracting Funding

Destination Tourism

Destination Tourism is simply what its name implies: visitor attractions and destinations that have established a favorable and widespread reputation. Such destinations can be beautiful or unusual natural features, cultural/historic sites, as well as man-made places such as resorts, amusement parks and casinos.

Frequently, community advocates have an inflated perspective about the reputation of their community as a visitor destination. If the community is not blessed with existing natural, cultural or historic assets, it may be challenged to establish itself in the mind of the traveling public without investing in the development of new facilities and attractions that position the community to attract travelers from hundreds—if not thousands—of miles away.

Destination travelers tend to expend more discretionary income daily than pass-through travelers do. As such, Destination Tourism is a more significant contributor to local economies.

There are three primary ingredients to a Destination Tourism strategy: the attraction itself, a well-run marketing organization and a competitive marketing budget. Without any of the three of these, a Destination Tourism strategy will likely fail.

> **Destination Tourism**
> ...is often the highest value tourism development strategy because it capitalizes on regionally or nationally recognized attractions. Such attractions draw a large number of visitors, many of whom spend more dollars than the average tourist.

In order to determine if a community has a viable Destination Tourism strategy, it is important to have a global perspective. Imagine yourself as a resident of a state 500 miles away. Would you view what your community has to offer as a "destination"? Would your tourism amenity motivate a family to plan a multi-day visit weeks, if not months, in advance? If not, perhaps you have an over-inflated view of the attraction in your backyard.

Another consideration is the impact of a Destination Tourism strategy. Communities that benefit from extended visitor stays tend to create a bifurcated economy. In other words, they tend to gravitate economically to the "haves" and the "have-nots" due to the uneven distribution of wealth generated from tourism economies. Such an outcome can have significant impacts on infrastructure, housing and social service delivery.

Examples of Strategic Implementation Activities

- Recruitment of a destination resort
- Casino development
- Providing access to an outstanding natural area
- Upscale lodges and hotels
- Theme parks

Advantages	Drawbacks
<ul><li>Significant investment and job creation</li><li>Elevating community image benefiting other strategies (especially Business Recruitment)</li></ul>	<ul><li>Increased traffic and congestion</li><li>Potential for bifurcated economy</li><li>Inflationary pressure on local housing</li></ul>

Key Success Factors

- Adequate housing for labor force
- Community acceptance of the visitor industry
- Local, available, high-skill labor pool
- Local, available, low-skill labor pool
- Local government support
- Proximity to nationally recognized attractions
- Proximity to scheduled air service
- Sophisticated tourism development and promotion
- Sufficient marketing, promotion or public relations budget

Cultural Tourism

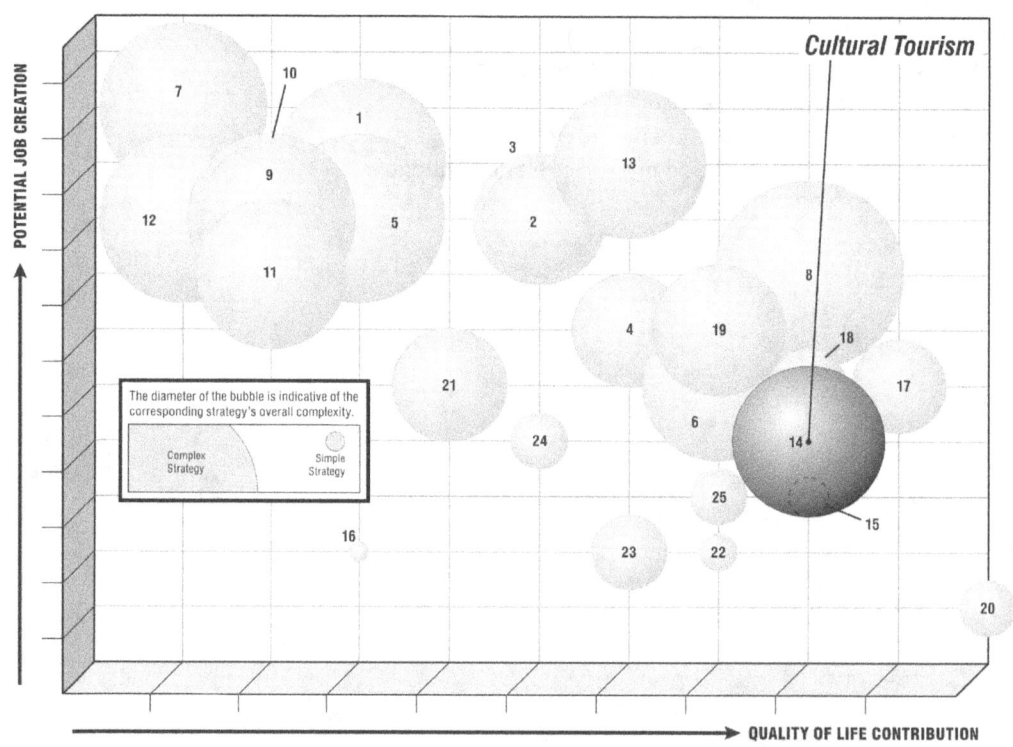

1. Business Recruitment
2. Business Retention & Expansion
3. Business Cultivation
4. Entrepreneurial Development
5. Energy Development
6. Environmental Restoration
7. Logistics Centers
8. Leading-edge Development
9. Value-added Agriculture
10. Value-added Forest Products
11. Value-added Fisheries
12. Value-added Mining
13. Destination Tourism
14. Cultural Tourism
15. Local/Regional Tourism
16. Pass-through Visitor Services
17. Downtown Development
18. Education Development
19. Health Care Expansion
20. Bedroom Community Development
21. Infrastructure Development
22. Attracting Retirees
23. Attracting Lone Eagles
24. Attracting Government Jobs
25. Attracting Funding

Cultural Tourism

Many communities have capitalized on local culture to create jobs. Cultural opportunities based on such human interests as dance, theater, music and distinctive food can help build the local economy.

In order to be successful with this strategy, a high standard of excellence must be set and pursued. People will travel from hundreds of miles away, for example, for an excellent Shakespearean Festival.

> **Cultural Tourism**
> ...relies on a community's capacity to provide visitors, especially from out-of-state, with high-quality experiences related to the arts, including performing and visual, local history and seasonal events such as large agricultural fairs.

The pursuit of a new cultural tourism attraction or element should not be undertaken without significant research into the prospective competitive advantages that the community would enjoy, and the long-term operational and marketing obligations required.

Quite obviously, the most important factor for a Cultural Tourism strategy is the availability—or potential availability—of the cultural attraction itself. A cultural attraction with a long-standing record of drawing visitors from hundreds of miles away presents a community with the opportunity to develop complementary services and facilities for community economic benefit.

In addition to the attraction itself, the community benefits from having an effective organization with a competitive marketing budget.

An advantage of a Cultural Tourism strategy can be the positive reputation that a community enjoys which can create collateral benefit for other strategies. Communities that are perceived to be sophisticated and centers of excellence can draw new residents and business activity based upon this reputation.

Examples of Strategic Implementation Activities	
• Expansion of an existing cultural attraction • Establishment of a new cultural attraction	
Advantages	**Drawbacks**
• Enhancement of community pride and support of local iconic events • Above average per-visitor expenditures	• Potential for economic benefits to be seasonal only
Key Success Factors	
• Cultural development and advocacy organization • Existing or prospective cultural attraction • Local, available, high-skill labor pool • Local, available, low-skill labor pool • Sufficient marketing, promotion or public relations budget	

Local/Regional Tourism

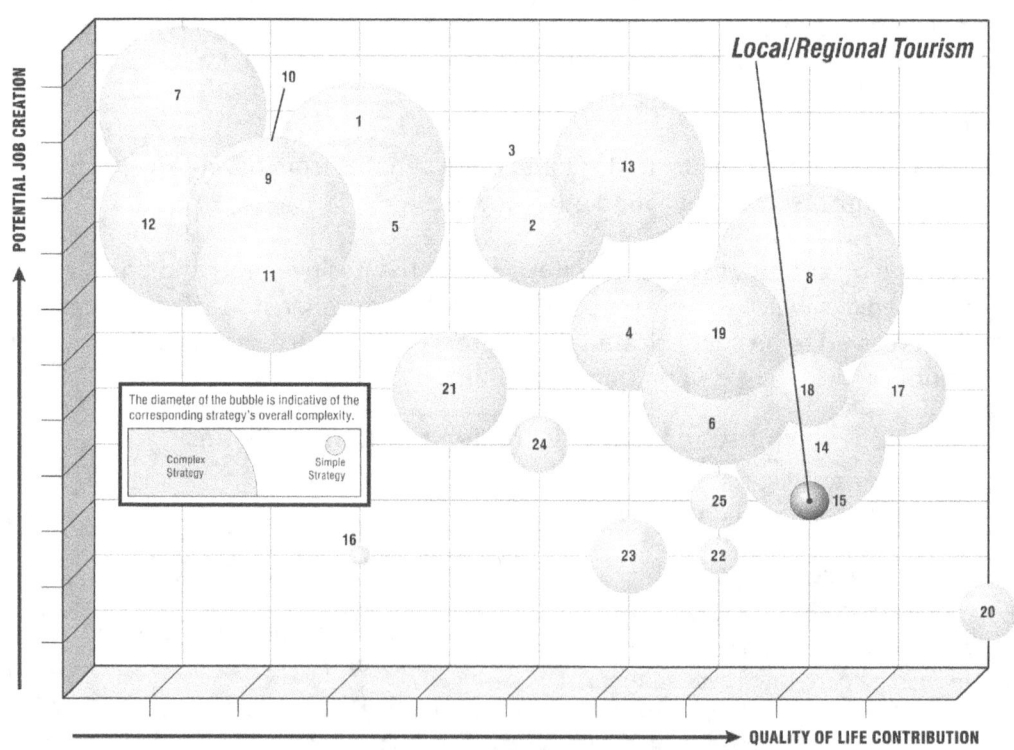

Local/Regional Tourism

POTENTIAL JOB CREATION

QUALITY OF LIFE CONTRIBUTION

The diameter of the bubble is indicative of the corresponding strategy's overall complexity.

Complex Strategy   Simple Strategy

1. Business Recruitment
2. Business Retention & Expansion
3. Business Cultivation
4. Entrepreneurial Development
5. Energy Development
6. Environmental Restoration
7. Logistics Centers
8. Leading-edge Development
9. Value-added Agriculture
10. Value-added Forest Products
11. Value-added Fisheries
12. Value-added Mining
13. Destination Tourism
14. Cultural Tourism
15. Local/Regional Tourism
16. Pass-through Visitor Services
17. Downtown Development
18. Education Development
19. Health Care Expansion
20. Bedroom Community Development
21. Infrastructure Development
22. Attracting Retirees
23. Attracting Lone Eagles
24. Attracting Government Jobs
25. Attracting Funding

Local/Regional Tourism

While most communities do not have a destination attraction in their backyard, they may have a recreational or historical/cultural asset(s) that can draw visitors within a day's drive and stimulate the local economy.

> **Local/Regional Tourism**
> ...is a strategy communities may pursue that does not have a destination attraction or significant cultural/historic/environmental assets but can provide events and other experiences that draw visitors from within the region.

Many communities have successful weekend events designed to celebrate the community's history and/or culture. These events have potential to draw people from at least a county or two away.

By investing in the local tourism "product" and marketing efforts, the value of tourism expenditures can be maximized.

Communities should understand that employing a Local/Regional Tourism strategy is not an economic panacea. Such a strategy can have a modest economic impact, however, and bolster community pride.

In order for a community to attract people in the region for a day trip, there must be one or more visitor attractions and/or events that can capture the attention individuals and families and motivate them to make the trip. Taking a realistic inventory of such attractions—and making their availability known to regional residents—is the key.

Virtually every "civic citizen" has a bias about how good their visitor attractions are. This comes with being a community citizen, and it is not necessarily bad. However, in order for a Local/Regional Tourism strategy to be successful, the community needs to have a competitive "attraction advantage" relative to its neighboring communities and counties. If this is not the case, resources and human energy can be wasted pursuing unrealistic expectations.

Examples of Strategic Implementation Activities
• Fostering business growth along travel corridors • Promotional and marketing activities that attract travelers • Development of motels, retail establishments and restaurants • Annual community events • Promotional budget to inform region of the event(s) • Development of a welcome center

Advantages	Drawbacks
• Enhancement of community pride • Improved community facilities for benefit to residents	• Dispersed and intermittent economic benefit

Key Success Factors
• Local recreational and visitor attractions • Relative sophistication in coordinating and marketing local events • Strong community support • Sufficient marketing, promotion or public relations budget

Pass-through Visitor Services

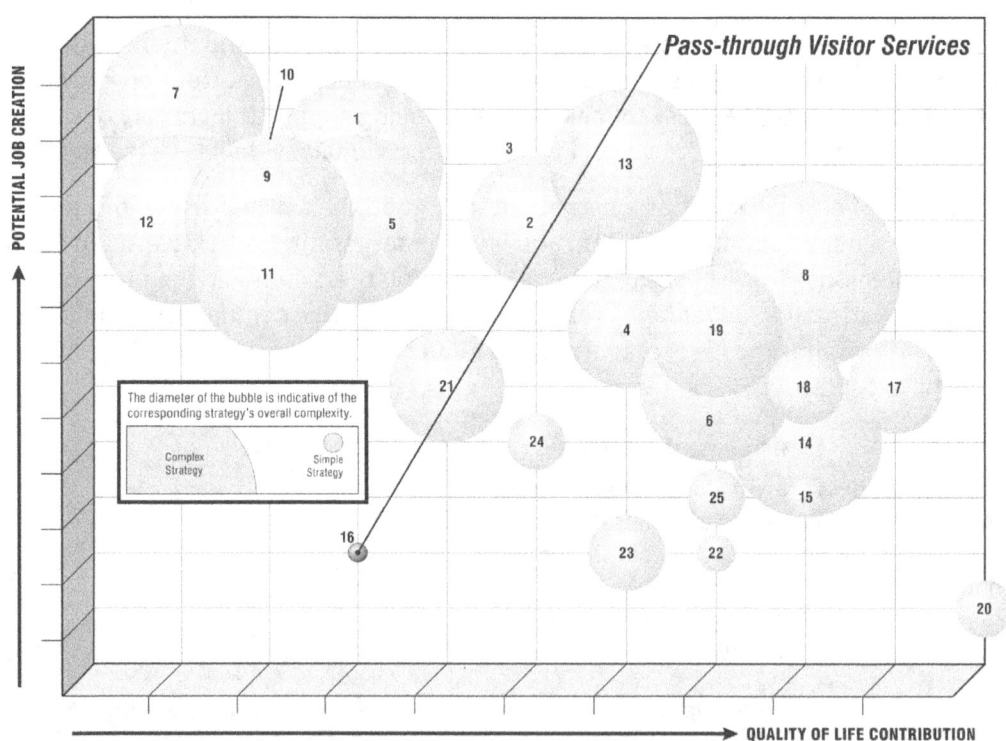

POTENTIAL JOB CREATION

Pass-through Visitor Services

The diameter of the bubble is indicative of the corresponding strategy's overall complexity.

Complex Strategy

Simple Strategy

QUALITY OF LIFE CONTRIBUTION

1. Business Recruitment
2. Business Retention & Expansion
3. Business Cultivation
4. Entrepreneurial Development
5. Energy Development
6. Environmental Restoration
7. Logistics Centers
8. Leading-edge Development
9. Value-added Agriculture
10. Value-added Forest Products
11. Value-added Fisheries
12. Value-added Mining
13. Destination Tourism
14. Cultural Tourism
15. Local/Regional Tourism
16. Pass-through Visitor Services
17. Downtown Development
18. Education Development
19. Health Care Expansion
20. Bedroom Community Development
21. Infrastructure Development
22. Attracting Retirees
23. Attracting Lone Eagles
24. Attracting Government Jobs
25. Attracting Funding

Pass-through Visitor Services

Depending on a community's proximity to major highways, scenic byways and other significant travel routes, communities can enjoy the economic benefit of non-destination visitor expenditures.

Travel expenditures can be categorized as destination travel expenditures or pass-through travel expenditures. Unlike destination travel, pass-through travel is simply the activity visitors engage in on the way to their ultimate destination. Related expenditures are typically for fuel, food and sometimes lodging.

> **Pass-through Visitor Services**
> ...is a strategy that may be used by communities to capture dollars spent by visitors for services they need and want on their way to other destinations.

Generally, these expenditures are made regardless of efforts by local communities. Some specific things, however, can have a modest impact on pass-through visitor expenditure patterns. These include

- Informational signage on travel routes (freeways, highways, etc.)

- Beautification of community entrances

- Low-frequency AM radio messages

- Hospitality training about local visitor attractions for front-line workers

- Expansion of businesses serving the travelling public

The obvious key factor for this strategy is "being at the right place at the right time"— either you have it or you don't.

In addition to the primary location factor, two other key factors are the willingness and ability of local leaders and business people to capitalize on the community's location, and the availability (or lack thereof) of the local labor force.

A Pass-through Visitor Services strategy has relatively little upside and probably no downside. While the wages and benefits may be negligible, and will probably be dispersed, it still can be a very important strategy for businesses that rely on visitor expenditures for revenue. Taking simple measures may have long-standing benefit.

Examples of Strategic Implementation Activities

- Fostering business growth along travel corridors
- Promotional and marketing activities that attract travelers
- Development of motels, retail establishments and restaurants

Advantages	Drawbacks
• Quietly generates modest benefits	• Relatively little—and very localized—economic benefit • Wages are typically low

Key Success Factors

- Local, available, high-skill labor pool
- Local, available, low-skill labor pool
- Local focus on revenues from visitors
- Proximity to travel routes

Downtown Development

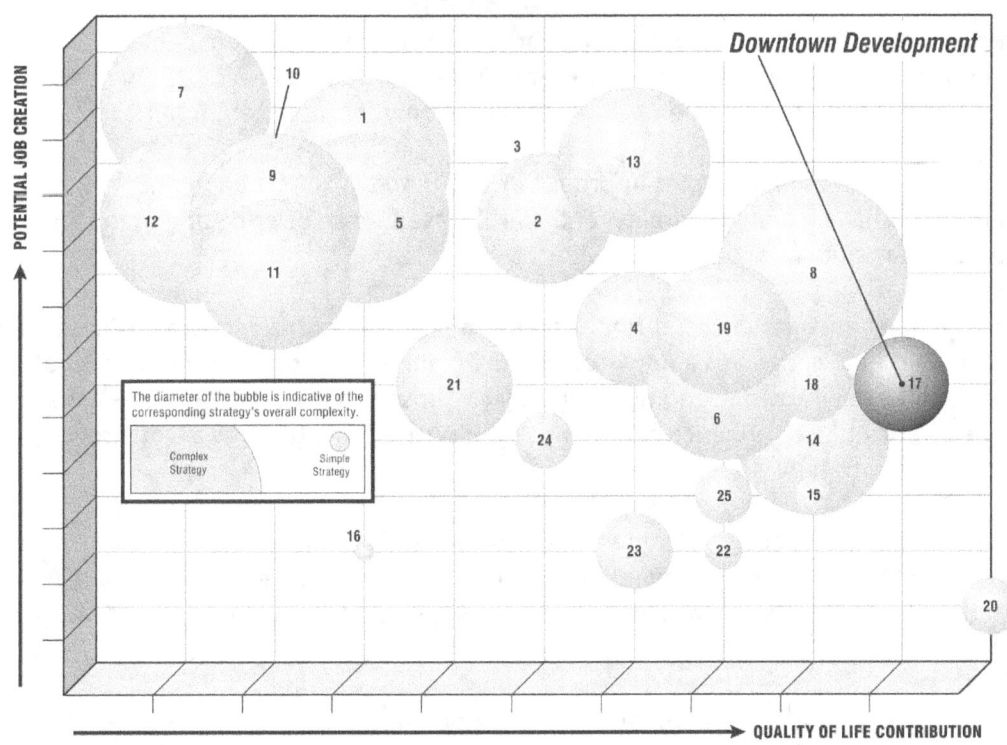

1. Business Recruitment
2. Business Retention & Expansion
3. Business Cultivation
4. Entrepreneurial Development
5. Energy Development
6. Environmental Restoration
7. Logistics Centers
8. Leading-edge Development
9. Value-added Agriculture
10. Value-added Forest Products
11. Value-added Fisheries
12. Value-added Mining
13. Destination Tourism
14. Cultural Tourism
15. Local/Regional Tourism
16. Pass-through Visitor Services
17. Downtown Development
18. Education Development
19. Health Care Expansion
20. Bedroom Community Development
21. Infrastructure Development
22. Attracting Retirees
23. Attracting Lone Eagles
24. Attracting Government Jobs
25. Attracting Funding

Downtown Development

Most communities have a central business district commonly referred to as their "downtown." Frequently, this area is recognized as the community's business center, and is the social and economic heart of the community.

The National Trust for Historic Preservation created the National Main Street Center Four-Point Approach for downtown advocacy. These points are

> **Downtown Development**
> ...includes a wide range of activities a community can undertake to preserve, develop and promote its downtown/central business district in order to increase business investment and activity.

- Organization (volunteers, staffing, board of directors)

- Promotion (events, public relations, advertising)

- Design (building and amenity stabilization, preservation, beautification)

- Economic Restructuring (supporting existing businesses; promoting new businesses)

Often ignored is the fact that downtowns are often large employment centers. While most downtown business activity may primarily serve other businesses, as well as residents, it is still a vital element of the local economy for most communities.

By capitalizing on the Four-Point Approach outlined above, jobs are created, communities have increased vitality, and an increased sense of pride and optimism is created and maintained.

Although many fast-growing suburban communities may not have a core business area commonly acknowledged as a downtown, most communities do. Communities that have a robust downtown economy—particularly those in a historical setting—have a unique opportunity to enhance community vitality and pride through a Downtown Development strategy.

In addition to a well-recognized downtown, other key factors for success include a well-run downtown development advocacy organization, as well as dedicated funding for both the organization's operations and the development/promotion of the downtown itself.

There are many benefits to a Downtown Development strategy that extend beyond the retention and creation of jobs. A most important one is the preservation of the heart and soul of many communities, which often is the primary basis of "community" itself.

While residents of a community often take their downtown for granted, newcomers to an area frequently form their first—and most important—impression of a community from the nature and character of its downtown. Consequently, similar to other strategies such as Business Recruitment, a Downtown Development strategy can produce long-term payoffs.

Examples of Strategic Implementation Activities
• Attraction of commercial and retail businesses • Building façade rehabilitation projects • Events and promotions • Development of community amenities and attractions

Advantages	Drawbacks
• Enhanced community pride • Creation of the "business card" supporting other strategies • Supporting local people (not generally out-of-town corporations)	• Job creation can be marginal and very dispersed (frequently not noticed) • People in businesses in other areas of the community may think the city is favoring downtown business and building owners

Key Success Factors
• Active engagement of downtown building and business owners • Downtown organization and staff • Implementation of National Main Street Four-Point Approach™ • Local funding for downtown development • Local government support • Recognizable central business district/downtown

Education Development

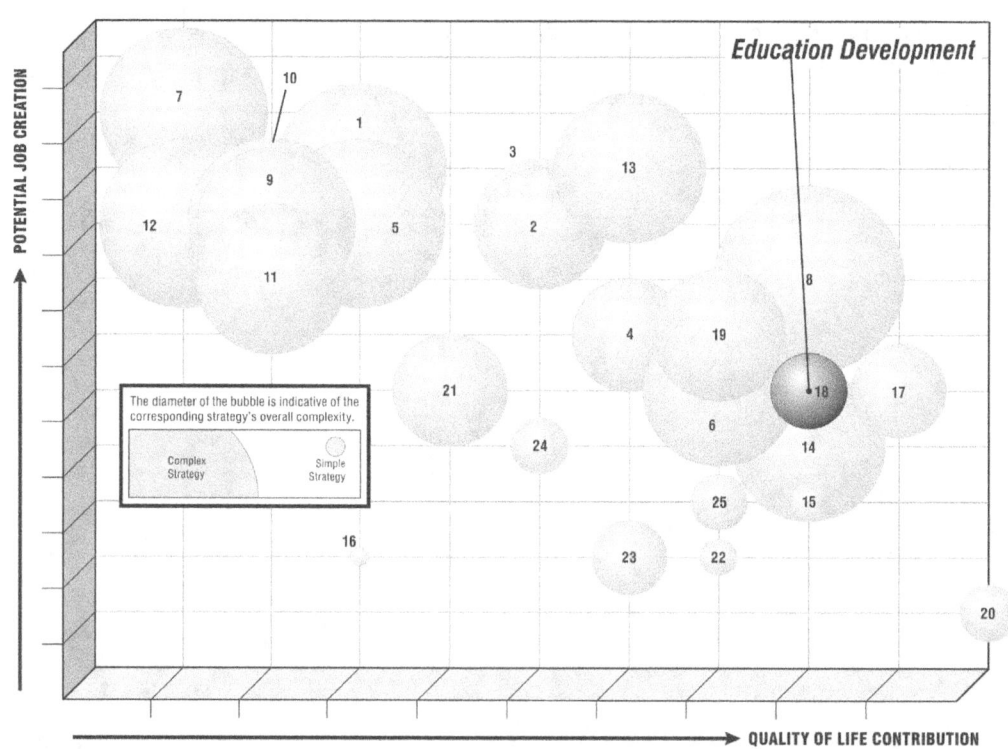

Education Development

POTENTIAL JOB CREATION

The diameter of the bubble is indicative of the corresponding strategy's overall complexity.

Complex Strategy   Simple Strategy

QUALITY OF LIFE CONTRIBUTION

1. Business Recruitment	7. Logistics Centers	13. Destination Tourism
2. Business Retention & Expansion	8. Leading-edge Development	14. Cultural Tourism
3. Business Cultivation	9. Value-added Agriculture	15. Local/Regional Tourism
4. Entrepreneurial Development	10. Value-added Forest Products	16. Pass-through Visitor Services
5. Energy Development	11. Value-added Fisheries	17. Downtown Development
6. Environmental Restoration	12. Value-added Mining	18. Education Development

19. Health Care Expansion
20. Bedroom Community Development
21. Infrastructure Development
22. Attracting Retirees
23. Attracting Lone Eagles
24. Attracting Government Jobs
25. Attracting Funding

Education Development

The provision of educational services, especially in rural communities, comprises a significant portion of the overall economy of a community. Communities that are home to community colleges, and especially to four-year higher education institutions, benefit from an even higher percentage of economic impact derived from provision of educational services.

Increasingly, the ability to earn a sufficient individual or family income is dependent upon educational attainment. Consequently, counties, states and regions that have a more educated population tend to compete better in the 21st century marketplace.

By developing a community development—and political—strategy to create or enhance the provision of educational services at all levels, communities can derive significant economic benefit. Further, pay for many jobs associated with the delivery of post-secondary educational services tends to meet the income requirements of most families.

> **Education Development**
> ...presents communities the opportunity to retain, upgrade and create jobs, including higher-paying jobs, by providing post-secondary education and training.

Such a strategy might simply entail the augmentation or expansion of existing post-secondary educational services. Alternatively, the strategy could be more ambitious such as the creation of an institute dedicated to researching and resolving emerging social or technologic issues, or the establishment of a four-year educational institution.

Communities desiring to pursue an Education Development strategy must be cognizant of the budget dynamics and emerging educational trends associated with the educational institution they are trying to attract/expand.

A community that desires to create jobs by retaining and recruiting students to the community may be best suited to approach an existing post-secondary institution (if there is one). In tight fiscal times, it may be difficult to influence the leadership of these institutions to "think outside of the box" and be open to considering expanding their services to meet community priorities.

Broad community support from a variety of sectors including government, business and education is an especially important factor for the success of this strategy. The availability of land and buildings, either on/near campus—or elsewhere in the community—is also a key factor that must be considered.

Communities may want to focus upon an educational or training niche that allows the community to gain a reputation for being a destination for a particular type of program or training. Simply competing to influence the very mature "education industry" may not make a convincing case for expanding or recruiting an educational institution.

The community may wish to examine existing business activity or location factors as a basis for determining and defining this educational niche.

Examples of Strategic Implementation Activities
• Recruitment of a branch campus of an existing educational institution • Expansion of an existing local educational institution • Establishment of a niche-specific training facility

Advantages	Drawbacks
• Above average wages • Captures potential of community-based talent pool • Peripheral benefit to other strategies such as Attracting Lone Eagles and Bedroom Community Development	• Subject to cyclical budget trends

Key Success Factors
• Advantageous location for government or education expansion • Cooperation of economic development staff and educational community • Expandable educational institution • Land/Buildings/Campus for education expansion • Local government support

Health Care Expansion

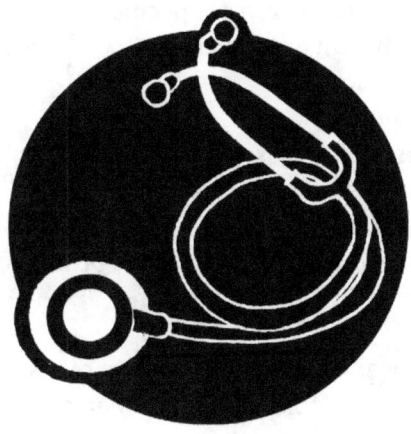

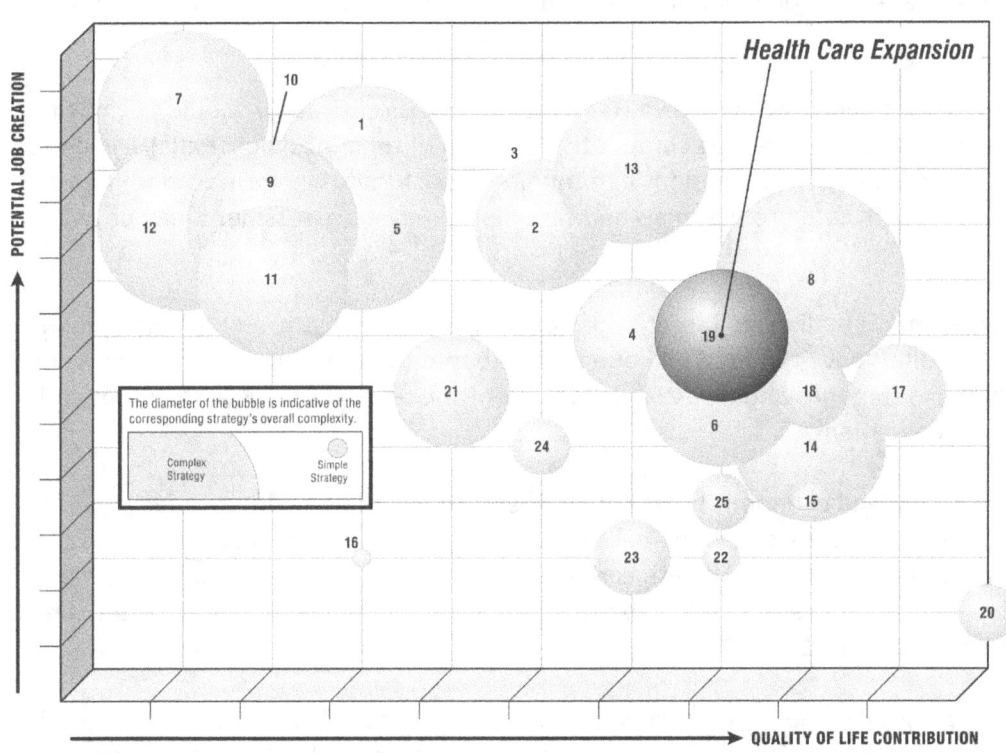

1. Business Recruitment
2. Business Retention & Expansion
3. Business Cultivation
4. Entrepreneurial Development
5. Energy Development
6. Environmental Restoration
7. Logistics Centers
8. Leading-edge Development
9. Value-added Agriculture
10. Value-added Forest Products
11. Value-added Fisheries
12. Value-added Mining
13. Destination Tourism
14. Cultural Tourism
15. Local/Regional Tourism
16. Pass-through Visitor Services
17. Downtown Development
18. Education Development
19. Health Care Expansion
20. Bedroom Community Development
21. Infrastructure Development
22. Attracting Retirees
23. Attracting Lone Eagles
24. Attracting Government Jobs
25. Attracting Funding

Health Care Expansion

Communities that have established notable centers of excellence for broad-based health care or specific health care specialties benefit from an unusually large cadre of well-paid professionals.

Communities such as Rochester, Minnesota, home of the Mayo Clinic, for example, benefit substantially from having a high health care *location quotient*. ("Location quotients" are an economic term referring the relative proportion of employment in an industry within a specific region.)

> **Health Care Expansion**
> … is a strategy communities may pursue to increase quality of life and to develop new health care-related jobs. The aging US population and increasing demand for more specialized services gives this strategy long-term viability.

National trends have a significant impact on health care, especially in rural communities. Mergers and acquisitions continue to create larger health care conglomerates that are controlling hospitals throughout the country. Additionally, federal policies on Medicaid and Medicare reimbursements have created a significant financial challenge for rural hospitals.

Communities desiring to pursue a Health Care Expansion strategy should begin with an objective analysis of the true competitive position of their local hospital(s)/clinic(s) and medical community. While many communities boast that they have competitively superior health care professionals and facilities, a realistic assessment may prove otherwise.

It may be more realistic to target a specialty area of health care. For example, many rural hospitals have targeted orthopedic care based upon the superiority of one or more orthopedic surgeons and investment in state-of-the-art orthopedic assessment and surgery equipment.

The business and economic health of an existing hospital or health care facility is of paramount importance in implementing a strategy designed to increase jobs through the provision of additional health care services. Hospitals that are struggling financially are generally not in a position to expand unless they can see an immediate and direct bottom-line benefit.

More specifically, the business acumen and entrepreneurial nature of the leadership team of the hospital/health care facility is critical. If the leadership team is strong, and has a focus beyond the confines of their organization, the community has an opportunity to advance a Health Care Expansion strategy.

A strong marketing budget, community support and available labor force are also important to the strategy.

The health care industry generally provides above-average wages. This, combined with potential opportunities stemming from potential industry-wide changes in health care services and delivery, can provide emerging opportunities to communities.

The passage of the Patient Protection and Affordable Care Act ("Obama Care") in 2010 has widespread implications for a Health Care Expansion strategy. The specific influence of the new federal health insurance program on this strategy is yet to be fully determined.

Examples of Strategic Implementation Activities
• Fostering the expansion of the existing hospital(s) and clinic(s) • Recruiting physicians • Targeting a sector (or multiple sectors) within the health-care field for growth

Advantages	Drawbacks
• Strengthens existing hospital and health care facilities • Above average wages • High-growth industry for foreseeable future	• Many health care business decisions are made outside the community

Key Success Factors
• Competent, strategic-minded hospital and health care executives • Existing excellence in local health care • Financially sound existing health care facility • Local, available, high-skill labor pool • Local, available, low-skill labor pool • Prospect of an expanded geographic market for health care • Strong community support • Sufficient marketing, promotion or public relations budget

Bedroom Community Development

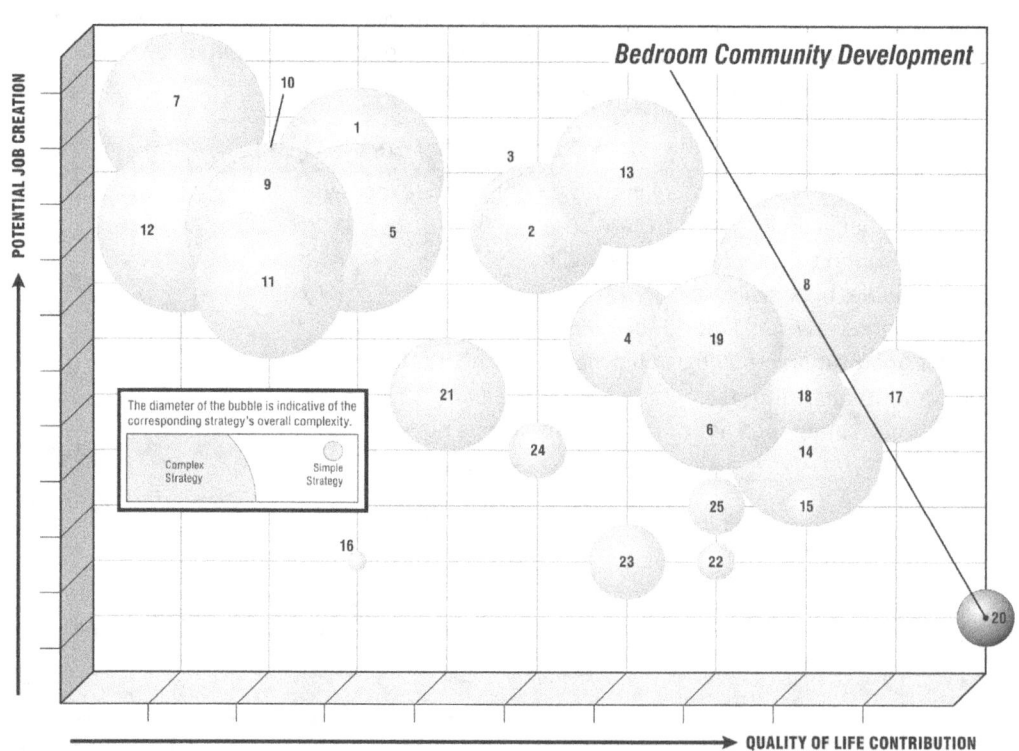

POTENTIAL JOB CREATION

Bedroom Community Development

The diameter of the bubble is indicative of the corresponding strategy's overall complexity.

Complex Strategy

Simple Strategy

QUALITY OF LIFE CONTRIBUTION

1. Business Recruitment
2. Business Retention & Expansion
3. Business Cultivation
4. Entrepreneurial Development
5. Energy Development
6. Environmental Restoration
7. Logistics Centers
8. Leading-edge Development
9. Value-added Agriculture
10. Value-added Forest Products
11. Value-added Fisheries
12. Value-added Mining
13. Destination Tourism
14. Cultural Tourism
15. Local/Regional Tourism
16. Pass-through Visitor Services
17. Downtown Development
18. Education Development
19. Health Care Expansion
20. Bedroom Community Development
21. Infrastructure Development
22. Attracting Retirees
23. Attracting Lone Eagles
24. Attracting Government Jobs
25. Attracting Funding

Bedroom Community Development

Many communities, particularly suburban ones, have established themselves—intentionally or not—as bedroom communities.

A "bedroom community" refers to a town or city that is largely absent of industrial and other basic industry activity. "Basic industry" refers to businesses that sell their goods and services largely outside of the local market area. Basic industry businesses are typically pursued by economic development professionals because they do more than simply circulate money and income within a community.

Urban areas and their suburbs have outperformed the rest of the nation economically over the past three decades. Consequently, many communities close to urban centers have experienced extraordinary housing construction and residential growth. As these communities become established and grow, public opinion favoring commercial and residential development, but not industrial development, often develops. A not-in-my-backyard (NIMBY) attitude forms.

> **Bedroom Community Development**
> ...is a strategy that recognizes the likely absence of many of the Key Success Factors needed to pursue other strategies but includes a focus on development of high-quality housing and provision of locally needed services.

A Bedroom Community Development strategy is unlike virtually all of the other strategies because it excludes the pursuit of some of the other strategies. For example, bedroom communities are unlikely to pursue Business Recruitment, Logistics Centers, value-added industry activity, and possibly even Business Retention and Expansion strategies.

While a Bedroom Community Development strategy might optimize real estate values, there are relatively few other economic benefits other than the preservation and enhancement of local quality of life.

The key factors for success for a Bedroom Community strategy are virtually opposite of the key factors for many other strategies, especially those weighted toward business development. Whereas most strategies require, for example, infrastructure and a strong business base, a bedroom community strategy does not. In fact, the lack of an industrial base is actually an advantage for this strategy.

Quality of life combined with proximity to other communities with a strong job base is the key for this strategy. Supportive local government policy and focus on residential land use codes is also advantageous.

For many communities, becoming a bedroom community is often more of a result than a planned effort. Nonetheless, communities that have evolved into bedroom communities can take measures to preserve this advantage in terms of focused business development activities and land-use practices that preserve housing values, minimize traffic congestion and provide parks and open space.

Examples of Strategic Implementation Activities	
• Designing high-quality housing subdivisions • Planning and development of rural residential property • Facilitation to support commercial businesses • Carefully managing any prospective industrial development	
Advantages	**Drawbacks**
• Sustained quality of life • Improved community amenities	• Restricts many other business development strategies • Potential escalation of home values (which can be viewed by some as an advantage)
Key Success Factors	
• Insulation from industrial business annoyances • Local policies and ordinances supporting quality neighborhood development • Proximity to urban population and workforce centers • Quality residential neighborhoods • Sufficient marketing, promotion or public relations budget	

Infrastructure Development

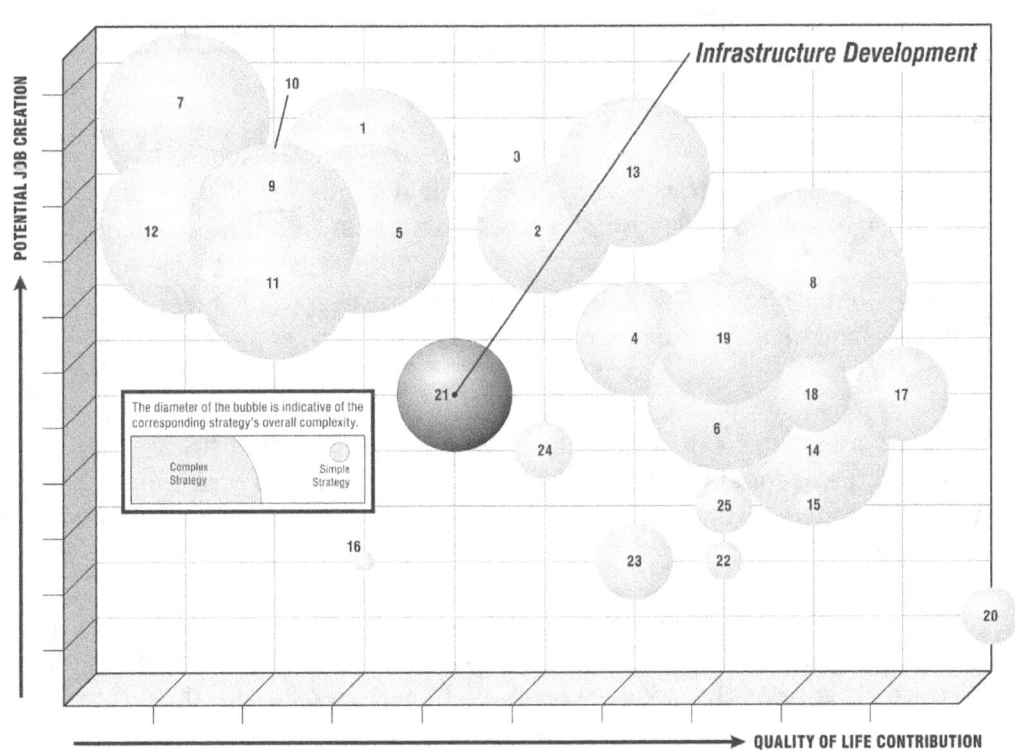

1. Business Recruitment	7. Logistics Centers	13. Destination Tourism	19. Health Care Expansion
2. Business Retention & Expansion	8. Leading-edge Development	14. Cultural Tourism	20. Bedroom Community Development
3. Business Cultivation	9. Value-added Agriculture	15. Local/Regional Tourism	21. Infrastructure Development
4. Entrepreneurial Development	10. Value-added Forest Products	16. Pass-through Visitor Services	22. Attracting Retirees
5. Energy Development	11. Value-added Fisheries	17. Downtown Development	23. Attracting Lone Eagles
6. Environmental Restoration	12. Value-added Mining	18. Education Development	24. Attracting Government Jobs
			25. Attracting Funding

Infrastructure Development

The term infrastructure is used here to describe all of the basic utilities and public services needed by communities and businesses. Infrastructure includes, but is not limited to, power, water, sewer, storm sewer, streets/roads and telecommunications.

Although Infrastructure Development is an economic development strategy, it is typically viewed as a means-to-an-end in terms of providing the necessary input for other strategies to be successful.

It is considered an economic development strategy because it is a long-term commitment toward the betterment of communities and the businesses they support.

Communities need to examine the infrastructure requirements of their current residents, as well as in terms of their projections of future residential, commercial and industrial demands.

> **Infrastructure Development**
> ...is a strategy that communities may use to invest in water, sewer, streets/roads and other infrastructure to encourage additional investment, create jobs, increase capacity and stimulate future desired development.

The federal government and most state governments provide long-term, low-interest debt financing to advance eligible infrastructure projects. At times, particularly when immediate job creation opportunities arise, grant funding is available for infrastructure development.

Communities pursuing an Infrastructure Development strategy should strategically assess their needs, and formulate solutions consistent with long-term projections.

Communities should also consider their location with respect to the federal government's (and their state's) possible desire to locate jobs in a geographically strategic manner.

Four factors combine to create a viable Infrastructure Development strategy: the ability to understand the needs and costs of infrastructure, the ability to access funding, the ability to mobilize a team of experts and the willingness of the community's leadership to think long-term.

Financing infrastructure is never fun—and it is never easy. Communities that have completed the necessary planning and have consistently matched their capital and maintenance expenses with incoming revenues are best prepared for the future. Unfortunately, it is all too easy to suspend solutions to these long-term problems. As a result, communities somewhat frequently must impose significant rate increases or pursue bond funding in order to catch up with deferred maintenance and compensate for political leadership that did not adequately address longer-term infrastructure requirements.

On one hand, it is difficult to categorize Infrastructure Development as an economic development strategy. As noted above, Infrastructure Development is typically only a means to an end. On the other hand, businesses seeking to expand or relocate will have specific infrastructure requirements and need them immediately. Communities that have prepared themselves for such business development opportunities stand a much higher likelihood of success with a variety of the other business development strategies.

Examples of Strategic implementation Activities
• Complete environmental assessment and/or environmental impact statements • Complete engineering and cost estimates • Identify and procure funding sources • Consider marketing strategies to promote increased land availability

Advantages	Drawbacks
• Broad, long-term benefit to community	• Short-term benefit may only be initial construction activity

Key Success Factors
• Access to long-term infrastructure loans and grants • Accurate, long-term analysis of infrastructure needs and costs • Community support for needed infrastructure rate increases • Team approach to financing infrastructure

Attracting Retirees

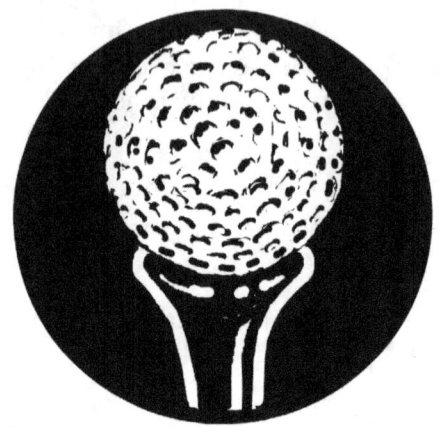

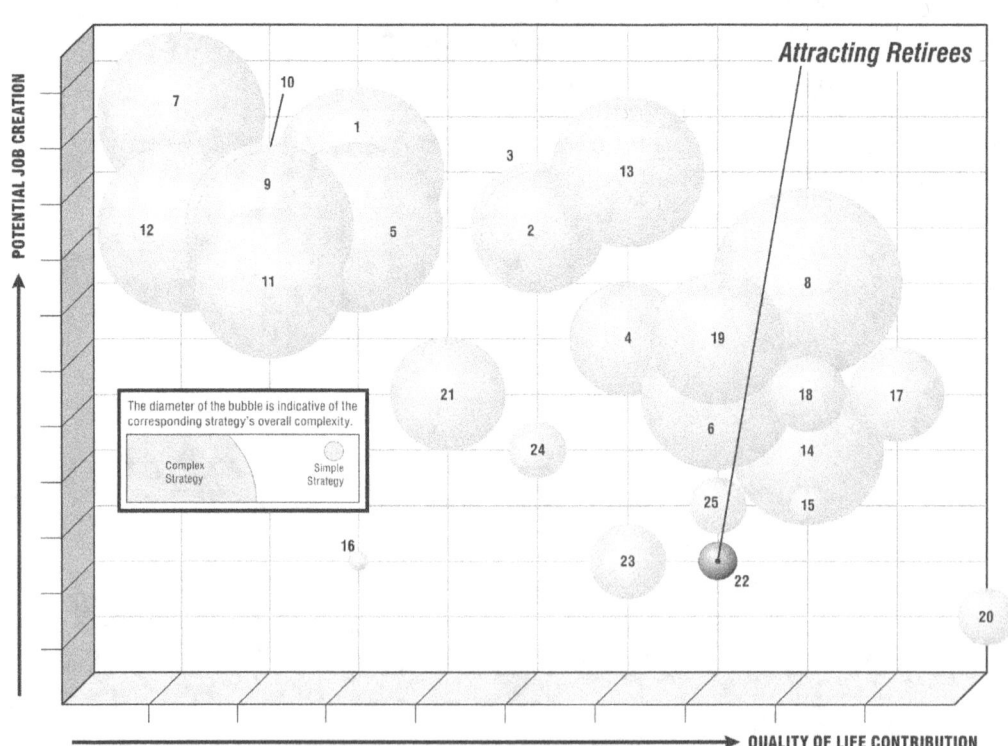

1. Business Recruitment	7. Logistics Centers	13. Destination Tourism	19. Health Care Expansion
2. Business Retention & Expansion	8. Leading-edge Development	14. Cultural Tourism	20. Bedroom Community Development
3. Business Cultivation	9. Value-added Agriculture	15. Local/Regional Tourism	21. Infrastructure Development
4. Entrepreneurial Development	10. Value-added Forest Products	16. Pass-through Visitor Services	22. Attracting Retirees
5. Energy Development	11. Value-added Fisheries	17. Downtown Development	23. Attracting Lone Eagles
6. Environmental Restoration	12. Value-added Mining	18. Education Development	24. Attracting Government Jobs
			25. Attracting Funding

Attracting Retirees

The aging of America is resulting in an increasingly larger population of older, often financially independent individuals looking for high quality of life in their communities.

These individuals may be looking for a new permanent place to live, or perhaps a location for a vacation home in which they may reside for several months each year (e.g., "snow birds" that go to the southwest US during the winter).

> **Attracting Retirees**
> ...presents communities that have climate and other quality-of-life advantages the opportunity to attract retirees as permanent or part-time residents who will spend all or a portion of their retirement income/savings locally.

High-amenity communities can employ marketing strategies to attract such retirees.

Key amenities include a desirable climate, available cultural and educational resources, quality housing, nearby scheduled air transportation, "urban" services, proximity to recreational opportunities, local business services and restaurants and an extraordinary quality of life.

One advantage of this strategy is to increase disposable income within a community without significantly increasing the demand on local services (education, infrastructure, etc.).

The contributing key factors are the presence of a critical mass of the amenities retirees expect, as well as a proactive organization with a competitive marketing budget.

Where do you want to retire? Communities that desire to differentiate themselves as a retirement community need to objectively assess the amenities that exist for their current population.

Retiree recruitment strategies typically are region-based. For example, many communities in the southwestern United States have become renowned as havens for year-round or part-time retirees.

Finally, communities desiring to recruit retirees need to give consideration to the social and economic dynamics that they bring. What effect, for example, will this strategy have on other strategies in the portfolio of the overall economic development strategic plan?

Examples of Strategic Implementation Activities

- Development of community facilities and amenities attractive to retirees
- Targeted marketing and public relations efforts
- Focus on increasing desirability of health care facilities
- Sector-specific housing development

Advantages	Drawbacks
<ul><li>Supports existing businesses and services</li><li>Generally draws wealthier people with more disposable income</li><li>Small impact on infrastructure</li></ul>	<ul><li>Dispersed and sometimes unnoticed economic benefit</li><li>Potential to be separate from existing, local social fabric</li></ul>

Key Success Factors

- Availability of urban services
- Available, desirable housing
- Desirable climate
- Existing excellence in local health care
- Existing recreational amenities
- Proximity to scheduled air service
- Staff focused on attracting retirees and/or lone eagles
- Sufficient marketing, promotion or public relations budget
- Support for attracting retirees

Attracting Lone Eagles

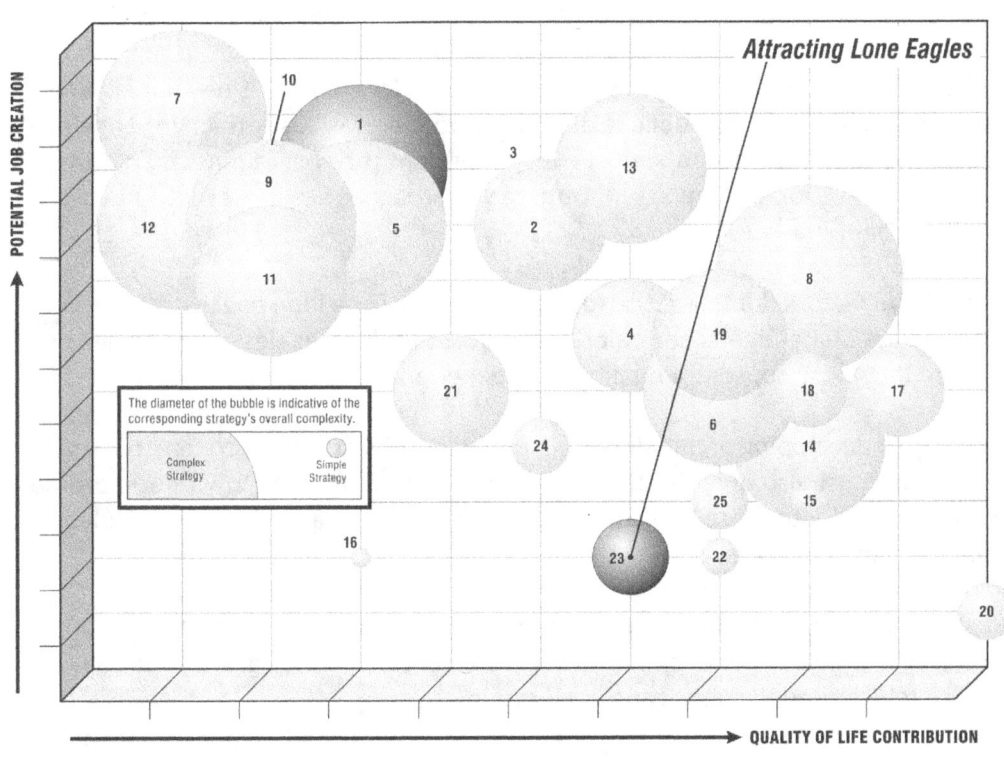

Attracting Lone Eagles

POTENTIAL JOB CREATION

QUALITY OF LIFE CONTRIBUTION

The diameter of the bubble is indicative of the corresponding strategy's overall complexity.

Complex Strategy

Simple Strategy

1. Business Recruitment
2. Business Retention & Expansion
3. Business Cultivation
4. Entrepreneurial Development
5. Energy Development
6. Environmental Restoration
7. Logistics Centers
8. Leading-edge Development
9. Value-added Agriculture
10. Value-added Forest Products
11. Value-added Fisheries
12. Value-added Mining
13. Destination Tourism
14. Cultural Tourism
15. Local/Regional Tourism
16. Pass-through Visitor Services
17. Downtown Development
18. Education Development
19. Health Care Expansion
20. Bedroom Community Development
21. Infrastructure Development
22. Attracting Retirees
23. Attracting Lone Eagles
24. Attracting Government Jobs
25. Attracting Funding

Attracting Lone Eagles

With improvements to the speed, sophistication and capacity of telecommunications infrastructure, an increasing number of small business owners that are location-independent can now operate their business virtually anywhere. Individuals who typically work alone and are highly dependent upon telecommunications have become known as lone eagles.

Attracting lone eagles to communities, particularly rural areas, has the advantage of bringing high-income, high-net-worth individuals into the community. Typically, these individuals have very low impact on infrastructure and other public amenities.

Similar to retirees, lone eagles look for quality-of-life factors such as access to recreation, historic and cultural attractions, local shopping, quality restaurants and business services.

> **Attracting Lone Eagles**
> ...is a strategy that recognizes many professionals and small businesses can locate almost anywhere they want because of increasing telecommunications capacity. The challenge is providing the amenities they expect.

A challenge many communities must meet to attract lone eagles is developing and employing a marketing and public relations program that is cost-effective. Lone eagles are typically mobile and found almost everywhere but the cost of mass marketing is usually prohibitive for communities. Targeted approaches are most cost-effective but miss the broader market.

Quality-of-life factors dominate the top requirements for a lone eagle strategy. In addition to adequate high-speed telecommunications, lone eagles, who can live nearly anywhere they want to, seek a quality living experience.

In addition to developing and maintaining the attributes attractive to lone eagles, communities must also organize themselves and commit funding toward the promotion of their community to these individuals. The convenient availability of scheduled air service is a significant plus.

If most of the needed conditions do not already exist, it may be difficult for a community to create an environment that is attractive for lone eagles, especially if adequate telecommunications capacity is lacking.

Attracting Lone Eagles can be a very appealing strategy because it has minimal impact on community infrastructure, yet it provides a significant up-side given the average income and local spending patterns of lone eagles.

Examples of Strategic Implementation Activities

- Targeted marketing and public relations efforts
- Efforts to ensure available high-speed Internet service
- Supporting the business viability of key ancillary services (business support, air service, etc.)

Advantages	Drawbacks
• High-income earners • Minimal impact on infrastructure	• Potential lack of engagement in civic life of community

Key Success Factors

- Availability of urban services
- Available, desirable housing
- Desirable climate
- Existing recreational amenities
- High-speed Internet
- Proximity to scheduled air service
- Staff focused on attracting retirees and/or lone eagles
- Sufficient marketing, promotion or public relations budget

Attracting Government Jobs

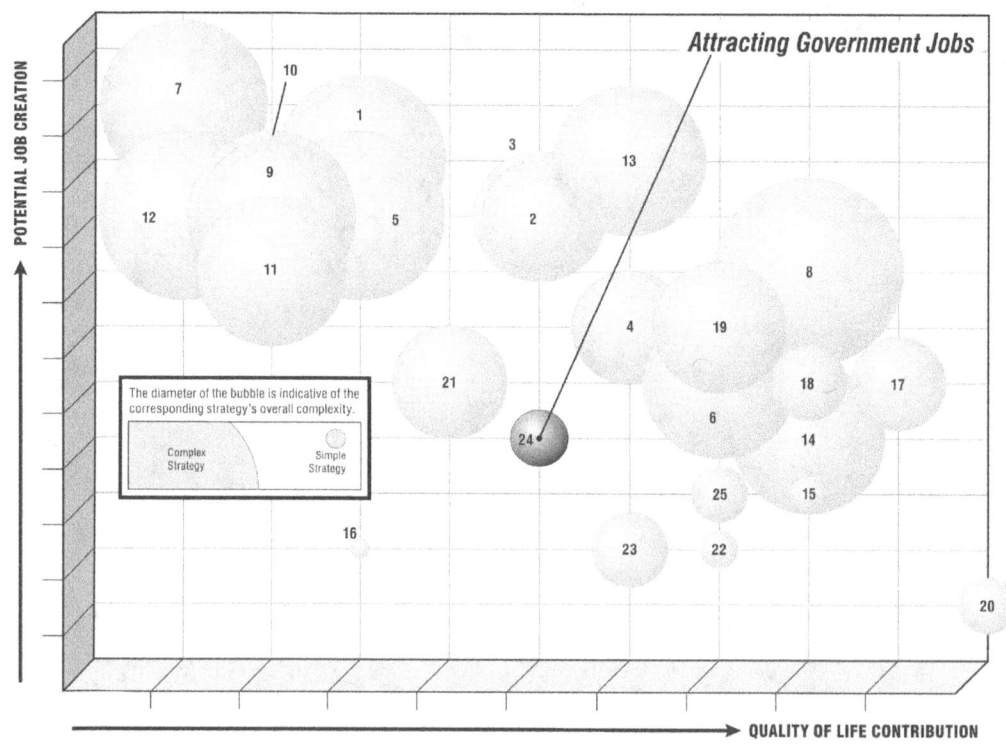

1. Business Recruitment	7. Logistics Centers	13. Destination Tourism	19. Health Care Expansion
2. Business Retention & Expansion	8. Leading-edge Development	14. Cultural Tourism	20. Bedroom Community Development
3. Business Cultivation	9. Value-added Agriculture	15. Local/Regional Tourism	21. Infrastructure Development
4. Entrepreneurial Development	10. Value-added Forest Products	16. Pass-through Visitor Services	22. Attracting Retirees
5. Energy Development	11. Value-added Fisheries	17. Downtown Development	23. Attracting Lone Eagles
6. Environmental Restoration	12. Value-added Mining	18. Education Development	24. Attracting Government Jobs
			25. Attracting Funding

Attracting Government Jobs

In most communities, particularly rural ones, government job wage levels far exceed median (often also referred to as "family wage") income levels. Accordingly, increasing the number of government jobs can provide a significant boost to the local economy.

In general (and particularly for rural communities), federal jobs pay more than state jobs; state jobs pay more than local government jobs; and local government jobs pay more than the community's average wages.

> **Attracting Government Jobs**
> ...presents communities an opportunity to attract and help state and federal agencies relocate or establish new offices/facilities in their area.

One significant factor in considering an Attracting Government Jobs strategy is the attitude of the local community toward such a strategy. Communities with a more conservative political viewpoint may shun such a strategy as being inconsistent with core beliefs.

Another key consideration is the trend line for the total number of government jobs. In times of economic recession, for example, many government jobs may be eliminated. On the contrary, during good economic times—or perhaps when a state is responding to a policy change that increases government jobs in one or more specific departments—communities can benefit by targeted government office recruitment strategies.

A strategy designed to create jobs by attracting the growth of state or federal government offices must be based on a realistic assessment of the budgetary trends of such offices. In addition to paying attention to the overall growth (or shrinkage) of government jobs at the state and federal levels, specific opportunities may emerge with agencies that are growing in response to current trends and policies.

Local efforts that not only include an understanding of trends in government staffing, but can employ sophisticated political approaches, stand the best chance for success.

Being aware of potential advantages based upon a community's location within the state can be beneficial. Local government support and available land and buildings can provide a comparative advantage.

Generally, state and federal governmental offices are not expecting approaches by local government and communities to encourage local job growth. It may take persistence by the community to generate openness to considering such a commitment by governmental officials.

Examples of Strategic Implementation Activities

- Recruitment of expanding state and/or federal agencies
- Development of land and buildings to foster the expansion of government jobs

Advantages	Drawbacks
• Above average wages • Stabilizing effect to local economy	• Potential community backlash, especially in rural areas

Key Success Factors

- Advantageous location for government or education expansion
- Availability of local buildings
- Availability of local land
- Capable, experienced economic development professionals
- Favorable state policies regarding office locations
- Local government support
- Projected growth in government budgets
- Strong community support

Attracting Funding

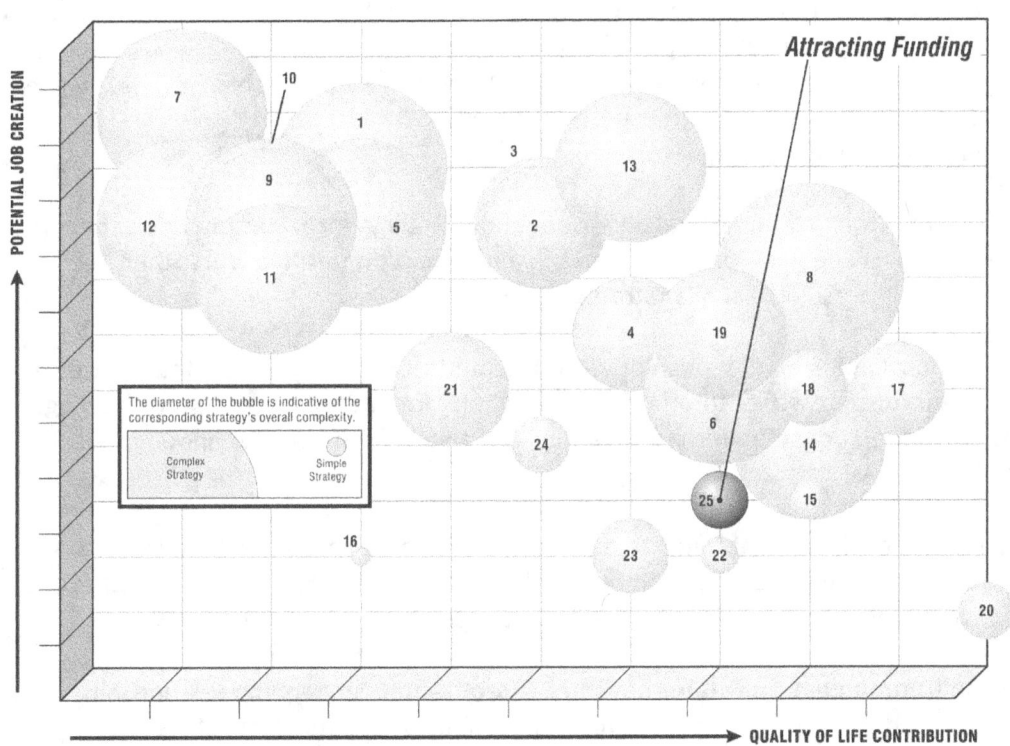

The diameter of the bubble is indicative of the corresponding strategy's overall complexity.

Complex Strategy | Simple Strategy

POTENTIAL JOB CREATION

QUALITY OF LIFE CONTRIBUTION

Attracting Funding

1. Business Recruitment
2. Business Retention & Expansion
3. Business Cultivation
4. Entrepreneurial Development
5. Energy Development
6. Environmental Restoration
7. Logistics Centers
8. Leading-edge Development
9. Value-added Agriculture
10. Value-added Forest Products
11. Value-added Fisheries
12. Value-added Mining
13. Destination Tourism
14. Cultural Tourism
15. Local/Regional Tourism
16. Pass-through Visitor Services
17. Downtown Development
18. Education Development
19. Health Care Expansion
20. Bedroom Community Development
21. Infrastructure Development
22. Attracting Retirees
23. Attracting Lone Eagles
24. Attracting Government Jobs
25. Attracting Funding

Attracting Funding

Communities can create jobs and improve their overall quality of life through either a onetime or continuing effort to attract government appropriations and grants, as well as foundation funding.

Hundreds of state and federal agencies manage grant programming and/or legislative earmarks (funding directives), which can be used to complete projects for a wide variety of purposes. States or localities with congressional representatives/legislators participating on powerful appropriations committees are particularly well positioned to benefit from this strategy.

While the vast majority of such funding is either for formula-based entitlement programs or for competitive grant processes, a small percentage is directed by state and federal appropriators, thus bypassing the formula or competitive approach.

Often maligned as "pork barrel spending," this strategy may face local opposition by individuals who are principled against such distribution of government funding. Additionally, recent changes in appropriations policy have significantly curtailed earmarked funding at the federal level.

> **Attracting Funding**
> ...is a strategy communities may use to secure money for economic and community development projects.

In order to attract state, federal and foundation funding, local community leaders must be able to package good projects/issues in a manner competitive with other communities pursuing a similar strategy.

Positive local political relationships with state and/or federal representatives are very important to successfully communicate and lobby for limited discretionary funding. Established relationships with foundations can also increase the likelihood of local funding success.

The current availability of funds to be appropriated or earmarked is also important. Obviously, such funding availability can ebb and flow depending upon the status of the governmental budget and the spending philosophy of the governing body.

Certain communities and states have benefited from long-standing relationships with powerful federal appropriators, resulting in billions of dollars of investment in infrastructure, public amenities and job creation. Communities in the states of Alaska and West Virginia, for example, were able to transform local economies for many years through this strategy.

Conversely, communities not fortunate to be represented by powerful, tenured appropriators have a significantly greater uphill battle to succeed with this strategy.

The political attractiveness of this strategy changes with the times. In good economic times, this strategy may be dismissed as "pork barrel spending," while in severe recessionary times this strategy is often more positively viewed as "economic stimulus."

Finally, it can be argued that Attracting Funding is not a strategy at all. Rather, Attracting Funding is simply a tactic or an "action step" necessary for the implementation of other strategies. As such, some communities may select the Attracting Funding strategy solely for the benefit of implementing other strategies in their strategic plan.

Examples of Strategic Implementation Activities	
• Packaging projects and issues for the attention of government and foundations • Developing positive relationships with state and federal appropriators and foundations	
Advantages	**Drawbacks**
• Immediate economic stimulus • Creation of infrastructure and facilities for long-term benefit	• Intermittent opportunities dependent upon the economy and governmental policy • Potential principled opposition to strategy at community level
Key Success Factors	
• Availability of appropriated funds • Local ability to identify and advance a funding proposal • Strong community support • Strong state and/or federal legislative delegation(s)	

BENEFITS AND COMPLEXITY OF STRATEGIES

It is helpful to consider three distinct characteristics of the 25 strategies:

- Potential for job creation

- Implications for quality of life

- Complexity of strategy implementation

Each of the 25 strategies has a unique capability to create jobs. Many of the business development strategies, for example, are pursued by communities for the singular purpose of job creation.

Similarly, each of the strategies has a distinct impact on a community's quality of life. Certain strategies—especially the strategies with a community development focus—are frequently implemented in part to enhance the quality of life for a community.

Finally, each of the strategies has a differing level of complexity with respect to the challenges of implementing the strategy itself. The likelihood that a community possesses specific Key Success Factors contributes to its strategy complexity. Typically, rural communities have fewer of the factors necessary to implement many of the strategies (especially business development strategies). Rural communities may wish to pay particular attention to strategy complexity when selecting strategies for implementation.

The extent to which each of the strategies contributes to job creation and quality-of-life for communities is shown in the bubble chart below. Each "strategy bubble" shows: 1) potential for job creation on the 'Y' axis, 2) potential for enhancing quality of life on the 'X' axis, and 3) the "complexity" of implementing the strategy by the relative size of the bubble.

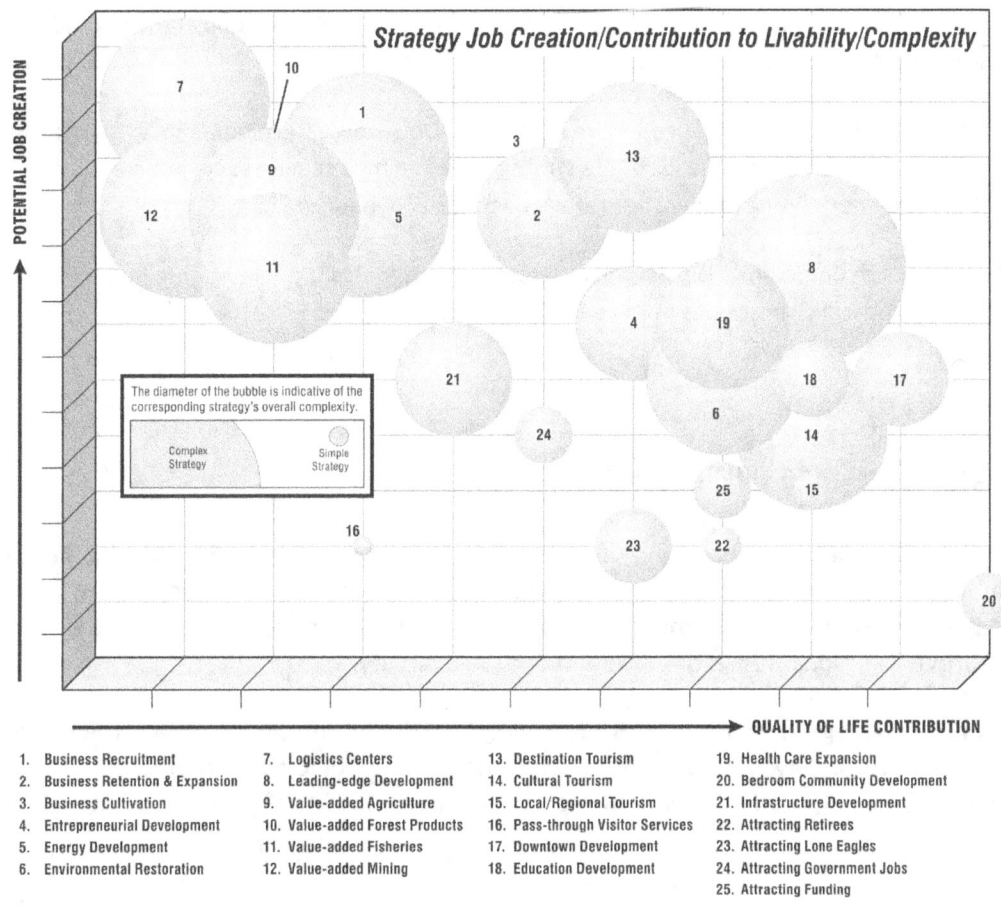

Strategy Job Creation/Contribution to Livability/Complexity

POTENTIAL JOB CREATION

QUALITY OF LIFE CONTRIBUTION

The diameter of the bubble is indicative of the corresponding strategy's overall complexity.

Complex Strategy   Simple Strategy

1. Business Recruitment	7. Logistics Centers	13. Destination Tourism
2. Business Retention & Expansion	8. Leading-edge Development	14. Cultural Tourism
3. Business Cultivation	9. Value-added Agriculture	15. Local/Regional Tourism
4. Entrepreneurial Development	10. Value-added Forest Products	16. Pass-through Visitor Services
5. Energy Development	11. Value-added Fisheries	17. Downtown Development
6. Environmental Restoration	12. Value-added Mining	18. Education Development

19. Health Care Expansion
20. Bedroom Community Development
21. Infrastructure Development
22. Attracting Retirees
23. Attracting Lone Eagles
24. Attracting Government Jobs
25. Attracting Funding

Key observations from the bubble chart include:

• High job-creation strategies tend to be lower quality-of-life producing strategies, and vice versa

• Strategies that have greater complexity tend to have a job creation and economic improvement focus

• One-third of the strategies are relatively high job-creators but must overcome significant complexity with respect to Key Success Factors and implementation challenges; this tends to favor urban areas

• Quality-of-life-focused strategies have lower job creation potential, and tend to have lower strategy complexity; rural communities tend to favor these strategies

• Business Retention and Expansion, Business Cultivation, Entrepreneurial Development, and Infrastructure Development show the potential for significant job creation with relatively low strategy complexity

• Leading-edge Development and Destination Tourism have the greatest combined jobs/livability benefit, but both strategies are very complex. Destination Tourism tends to have a high-wage/low-wage split.

• Health Care Expansion, Education Development, Downtown Development, and Attracting Funding tend to be high quality-of-life strategies, while maintaining some job creation benefits and exhibiting moderate strategy complexity dynamics

• A Bedroom Community Development strategy has significant quality-of-life benefits but does not typically contribute to job creation objectives

QUALITY-OF-LIFE INITIATIVES

Unlike the 25 strategies above that are a finite set of options for towns, tribes, cities and counties to improve their economy and livability, Quality-of-life Initiatives are an unlimited "open book." Communities can identify a wide variety of initiatives designed to improve their local sense of place and overall livability.

Also unlike strategies, there is no "Initiatives Wheel." Communities are free to define as many initiatives in any way they want. Therefore, the list below, presented alphabetically, only includes some of the most frequently identified and implemented initiatives.

Selection and implementation of Quality-of-life Initiatives is less strategic than selecting and implementing strategies. While Key Success Factors are presented below, these factors are less "mandatory." That is, communities can successfully implement their initiatives without such factors being comparative advantages. With Quality-of-life Initiatives, the *will* of the community may be all it takes.

Buy Local Campaigns

Many communities conduct "buy local" campaigns to encourage local residents to shop at businesses and stores that are locally owned. Such efforts not only support existing local businesses, but they preserve the sense of place within a community by supporting options to national chains that increasingly dominate the retail marketplace.

These campaigns can be as simple as regular public service announcements encouraging people to buy local, or more complex, including regular events that motivate people to seek out and patronize local businesses.

The local economy benefits by keeping local dollars supporting local businesses. While the overall economic benefits may be modest, the effort has the added value of providing encouragement to local entrepreneurs striving to grow their businesses.

Examples of Strategic Implementation Activities	
• Buy local campaigns • Routine events encouraging buy local activity	

Advantages	Drawbacks
• Keeps and circulates local dollars in the local economy • Supports local entrepreneurs	• Potential for only modest benefit from considerable effort

Key Success Factors	
• Local organization focused on buy local campaign • Public relations budget • Willingness of local citizenry to shop locally	

Child Care/Day Care

For some communities, particularly fast-growth ones, the availability of day care services is a quality-of-life matter. For families who cannot find such services, consequent restrictions on jobs and occupations become a surprising challenge to their way of life or even their ability to live in a particular community.

Examples of Strategic Implementation Activities	
• Governmental programs to subsidize day care • Funding for new day care facilities • Training programs for day care delivery	

Advantages	Drawbacks
• Supports family lifestyles • Supports labor force for businesses	• Market forces usually satisfy most communities without proactive measures

Key Success Factors	
• Available funding to subsidize day care operations or facilities • Local and/or state government support for day care • Market for day care services	

Civic Engagement

The truest sense of community is derived from people who truly care about one another and desire to positively engage to solve problems and celebrate their collective lives.

Yet the advent of television and other personal entertainment options such as iPods and personal computers has created a society where large community gatherings are typically reserved only for sports events and periodic celebrations. In the meantime, people are unplugging from their communities.

Good public policy stems from good community engagement. In today's society, this only happens through well-organized, proactive effort.

Examples of Strategic Implementation Activities
• Community leadership development programs
• Community forums
• Voter registration drives
• Community celebrations
• Use of online civic engagement tools

Advantages	Drawbacks
• Enhances sense of community • Improves community safety	• Difficulty of getting attendance at engagement events

Key Success Factors
• Local leadership focused on civic engagement
• Support from local media for civic engagement

Community Beautification

People should be proud of where they live. All too often, however, signs of apathy about the community's appearance are everywhere.   Litter lines the streets and highways. Graffiti defaces fences and buildings. Commercial storefronts have broken or boarded up windows. Salvage yards are located at city entrances. Such conditions are a clear statement about the community itself, and discourage business investment.

Beyond being unattractive, these degraded places in some communities become unsafe and undesirable, which fosters crime and illegal drug activity.

Well-organized and executed beautification efforts can begin small, yet have large payoffs. Small successes beget bigger efforts to improve the overall appearance and functionality of a community.

Examples of Strategic Implementation Activities
• Litter patrols
• Adopt-a-street program
• Community entrance signage
• Way-finding signage
• New clean-up ordinances
• Community clean-up days

Advantages	Drawbacks
• Increases community pride • Increases local safety • Facilitates business investment	• Need for substantial volunteer commitment

Key Success Factors
• Commitment by local citizens to clean up and enhance the appearance of the community
• Local government commitment

Community Center

Communities benefit from an all-purpose facility that can serve multiple functions, all stemming from the need for people to convene for social and/or community purposes. Generally referred to as a "community center," such facilities can serve multiple purposes, including as a senior center, a youth center or a general meeting facility.

For very small, rural communities, it is not unusual for this type of facility to serve many functions—from weddings to funerals and everything in between.

Examples of Strategic Implementation Activities	
• Community center • Civic center • Senior center • Youth center	
Advantages	**Drawbacks**
• Improves sense of place • Increases ability to draw large groups together • Provides efficient use of space for multiple groups and purposes	• Community facilities are generally not financially self-supporting
Key Success Factors	
• Available funding for development and maintenance • Available land/location for center • Community support for center • Local entity capable of assuming financial and maintenance responsibilities	

Emergency Medical Services
Depending upon the size of the community, the provision of emergency medical services may be a combination of funded, professional services and trained volunteer services. Such services are provided by city and rural fire departments, ambulance companies and sometimes, search/rescue organizations.

In rural communities, many of these services are provided by volunteers who not only must maintain training credentials, but volunteer their time in order to secure funding for equipment and facilities.

Examples of Strategic Implementation Activities
• Construction of new EMS facilities • Purchase of EMS equipment • Training for volunteers and professionals

Advantages	Drawbacks
• Enhances sense of community • Improves citizen safety	• Facilities and equipment are expensive

Key Success Factors
• Adequate base of professionals and/or volunteers • Adequate funding for equipment and/or facilities • Local government support for EMS programs and services • Supportive general public to invest in EMS services

Energy Conservation

Energy conservation projects such as retrofitting public buildings with better windows and insulation is a win-win for public agencies seeking to create short-term jobs and benefit the environment and financial bottom line over the long-term.

For many communities, pursuing energy conservation initiatives is a natural proactive measure to meet economic and environmental goals.

Examples of Strategic Implementation Activities
• Retrofitting public facilities • Providing financial incentives for building retrofit • Collaborating with electric utilities on energy conservation programs

Advantages	Drawbacks
• Stimulates short-term job creation • Provides long-term environmental benefits • Creates long-term financial benefits by lowering energy costs	• Net benefits of the program/initiative may not be seen for several years.

Key Success Factors
• Available public funding for energy conservation • Local expertise to advance conservation programs • Supportive local government for energy conservation

Homelessness

Over 600,000 people are homeless in America.

Communities take differing measures to address this problem locally. Local government, non-profits and religious institutions frequently work to address the problem through programs and shelters. Cities create policies and ordinances to help manage the challenging problem; working to support the homeless while addressing broader societal needs.

Driven by compassion for the homeless, as well as the desire to make the community as comfortable as possible for all, efforts to address the chronic problem of homelessness are certain to remain critical for many communities for the foreseeable future.

Examples of Strategic Implementation Activities	
• Homeless shelters • Food pantries and programs	

Advantages	Drawbacks
• Advances a compassionate society • Creates better living conditions for the homeless • Creates a safer environment for all • Improves business climate	• A belief that no matter what is done homelessness will continue • Dedicated financial resources needed

Key Success Factors
• Available funding for facilities and programs for the homeless • Community support for programs for the homeless • Local government leadership to address problem

Housing

Without question, one of the most important quality-of-life factors for any community is its housing supply. The specific issues that relate to satisfactory housing generally fall into one or more of three categories: affordability, availability and quality.

Housing affordability is an increasing problem given the widening income gap between rich and poor in America. Some communities, especially ones in and near popular tourism areas, face extreme situations where many low-income people have to travel long distances to work because housing is simply unaffordable.

In fast growth areas, the lack of available housing can be a severe problem. Strategies to build new housing to suit all income categories are challenging to implement.

Other communities may not be facing affordability and availability issues but desire to proactively develop housing as a significant contributor to overall local quality of life.

Communities and regions may have housing councils or authorities chartered to address these matters. Every state has a housing agency that passes through federal resources, as well as oftentimes manages state-specific resources for housing development.

Advancement of this initiative may depend on the political orientation of the community. Some communities do not desire to advance affordable housing projects because they are concerned that such developments only serve to increase the type of housing and associated activity that they find undesirable.

Other communities believe that one role of government and society at large is to proactively serve the less fortunate, and that housing is a basic human necessity.

All communities have some resources available to them given the fairly substantial role the federal government plays in supporting housing development and fair housing practices nationwide.

Examples of Strategic Implementation Activities	
• Establishment of housing council/ authority • Coordinated pursuit of housing funding and other resources • Creation of neighborhood design standards	
Advantages	**Drawbacks**
• Improves neighborhoods • Supports development of housing for people of all income levels • Increases social equity	• Potential large outlay of funding for perceived narrow benefit
Key Success Factors	
• Availability of financial resources for housing development • Available land for new housing development • Community support for housing projects • Existing housing stock • Local expertise to advise homeowners and renters, and advance housing initiatives • Private housing developers interested and capable of investing	

Local Foods

America is returning to its roots as many people are now seeking healthy, authentic local foods. After decades of big business setting and dominating the eating and dining trends of Americans, people are increasingly buying local, fresh foods.

While the trend may yet only be short-term in the overall food consumption pattern of the nation, for certain communities this initiative is not only about overall quality of life, but about finding healthier alternatives to diet patterns that are leading to obesity and other health issues.

Examples of Strategic Implementation Activities	
• Local farmers' market • Local stores carrying local agricultural products • Healthy eating information campaigns	
Advantages	**Drawbacks**
• Improves local health • Provides economic benefits for area agricultural producers and sellers	• Substantial volunteer support generally needs to be harnessed for this initiative
Key Success Factors	
• Access to quality produce and other local food products • Community support for local foods initiatives • Local coordinating expertise for farmers' markets and events	

Pet Shelters

Communities frequently find a need to address the problem of stray or unwanted animals. Without such initiatives, not only can the peace and tranquility of neighborhoods be negatively impacted, but health and safety issues can arise. Additionally, the community faces the unwanted issue of unnecessary cruelty to the animals.

Communities can mobilize through volunteer groups and/or organized/funded programs to address this problem. Such efforts can be as simple as caring people tending to the stray pets until longer-term solutions can be found, or as complicated as funding and operating a pet shelter.

Examples of Strategic Implementation Activities	
• Organizing a pet friends organization • Building and maintaining a pet shelter • Establishing new pet/other animal ordinances • Increasing law enforcement resources for animal control	
Advantages	**Drawbacks**
• Increases community peace and tranquility • Creates opportunity for animal lovers to address problem • Improves community health and safety • Improves conditions for animals	• Long-term human and financial resources are required
Key Success Factors	
• Adequate financial resources for facilities and operations • Community support • Local animal welfare advocacy group or organization	

Public Safety

The provision of public safety by cities and counties is considered a basic service of local government. Staffing and equipping local law enforcement is unquestionably one of the top priorities for these entities.

While crime has generally been on the decline in America for the past 20 years, there are still times when a city or county finds the need to reach beyond the traditional role of funding, staffing and maintaining local law enforcement services.

Communities that either are experiencing rapid growth, or have existing high crime rates, clearly know that crime reduces their quality of life.

Communities can employ non-traditional, crime-fighting measures such as Neighborhood Watches and other public campaigns to heighten the citizenry's awareness and capacity to fight crime.

Examples of Strategic Implementation Activities	
• Neighborhood watch campaigns • Crime fighters'	
Advantages	**Drawbacks**
• Improves community safety • Improves sense of place • Improves business climate	• Additional public funding is usually needed
Key Success Factors	
• Available local funding for crime prevention • Community resolve to address crime problem	

Public Transit

Many cities have public transportation systems. Larger cities may have underground subways or routed bus transportation systems. Smaller cities may have dial-a-ride services. In any event, communities frequently recognize that they have a responsibility to help their citizens with their mobility needs through public transportation systems.

Rural communities generally do not have bus service on established routes but sometimes they support the low-income population by developing on-demand public transportation.

Public transportation makes an important contribution to providing and maintaining vitally needed and efficient transportation systems. America's dependence on the automobile has largely defined the shape and much of the functioning of our communities. Maintaining the functionality and cost-efficiency of the transportation system frequently requires a public investment in transit.

Examples of Strategic Implementation Activities
<ul><li>Bus routes</li><li>On-demand public transit</li><li>Paratransit (specialized door-to-door transport service for disabled people)</li><li>Subways</li><li>Local taxi/van service</li></ul>

Advantages	Drawbacks
<ul><li>Provides low-income people with transportation services</li><li>Reduces use of automobiles</li><li>Environmental benefits from less traffic</li></ul>	<ul><li>Public transportation requires a financial commitment from local government</li></ul>

Key Success Factors
<ul><li>Available long-term funding for public transit</li><li>Local expertise/entity advocating and coordinating public transit</li><li>Local government support for public transit</li></ul>

Recreational Programs and Facilities

For many people, the availability of facilities and programs that provide recreation and promote fitness and overall wellness is very important. For many years, organizations such as the YMCA, YWCA and the Boys' and Girls' Clubs have coordinated programming and maintained facilities that allow local people to maintain a higher standard of health and fitness.

The lack of such programs and facilities contributes to a lower standard of health and lower overall enjoyment for the local citizenry.

Examples of Strategic Implementation Activities
<ul><li>Establishment of new health/fitness organization</li><li>Funding of new community fitness facilities</li><li>Expansion of programming for health, fitness and sports</li></ul>

Advantages	Drawbacks
<ul><li>Increases community pride</li><li>Improves health of the citizenry</li><li>Improves sense of place</li></ul>	<ul><li>Funding must not only be in place for developing programs and facilities, but also for continuing operations and maintenance</li></ul>

Key Success Factors
<ul><li>Community support for recreation programs and facilities</li><li>Local expertise to develop programs</li></ul>

Retail Development

Conventional economic theory holds that retail development is not an economic development strategy, but rather a result of a sound economy. If the expansion of basic industry and businesses that import wealth and export goods and services thrive, retail development will follow.

This is not always the case, and certain communities seek to recruit specific retail enterprises for economic and/or social reasons.

Another benefit of retail development for some communities/states is the incremental sales tax income that supports basic government operations.

Examples of Strategic Implementation Activities	
• Retail recruitment activities • Entrepreneurial and franchise development strategies	
Advantages	**Drawbacks**
• Increases local shopping opportunities • Increases community pride • Creates sales tax income for municipalities	• Potential redistribution of existing community wealth and jobs
Key Success Factors	
• Availability of local retail expenditure information • Available land and/or buildings for retail • Local expertise for retail recruitment	

Roads and Streets

One of the primary functions of city and county governments is providing and maintaining roads and streets (and highways for states and the federal government). For many communities, quality of life relates to successfully keeping up with the demands of meeting transportation needs with declining local budgets.

In addition to meeting current demand and maintaining past investments, some growth communities also need to proactively address the land purchase, design and construction of new neighborhoods. Developing standards that ensure cost-sharing of such infrastructure (including roads and streets) with developers is a key consideration.

Cities and counties have been squeezed financially for decades. The ability to maintain adequate funding for transportation infrastructure becomes more challenging every year.

Communities that fall behind with transportation infrastructure investment, however, eventually will have such liabilities catch up with them.

Examples of Strategic Implementation Activities
• Creation of area-wide levy to fund improvements • Development and adoption of design standards • Long-term master planning

Advantages	Drawbacks
• Meets current and future community needs • Avoids falling behind the infrastructure investment curve	• Streets and roads are expensive to build and maintain

Key Success Factors
• Long-term available funding for streets and roads • Local expertise to design and build streets and roads • Community support for infrastructure investment

Walking Paths and Trails

Communities often find that they have an asset right in the middle of the town. Sometimes cities and towns have a river or a former rail right-of-way that has existed for decades but now presents a new opportunity for a dedicated right-of-way for a trail or path system.

As America developed and expanded, it did so by capitalizing on access to rivers and to rail. Today, these historic assets often present themselves as a new possibility—miles of potential trails and bicycle paths adding to the livability of communities.

As communities seek ways to improve overall livability, the development of such recreational assets is an obvious choice when such resources are present.

Examples of Strategic Implementation Activities
• Rails-to-trails project • Riverfront trail/path development • Bicycle trail/path system development

Advantages	Drawbacks
• Enhances community livability • Increases community physical health and fitness	• Gaining ownership of right-of-way is often expensive and time consuming

Key Success Factors
• Availability of riverfront or other possible land right-of-way • Capability of community to plan and fund such recreational development • Community support for trail/path development

Workforce Development

The single-most important Key Success Factor for business development success in communities is the availability of a local labor pool that can meet the needs of existing and potential employers.

More than any time in our nation's history, workforce skills are critical to employment and income potential. The ability of nations to be competitive in a global economy is also increasingly dependent upon the skills of the labor force.

Given all this, communities frequently seek to advance initiatives to increase and enhance the skill base of the local labor force. This is often done in conjunction with local community colleges and four-year, post-secondary institutions.

Examples of Strategic Implementation Activities	
• Workforce development initiatives • Workforce Investment Boards	
Advantages	**Drawbacks**
• Progressive communities enhance civic engagement by working in partnership with local citizenry to bolster the local economy	• The needs of employers and the workforce are many, creating challenges to fully address the scope of the problem
Key Success Factors	
• Available funding for workforce development programs • Community focus on workforce development skills • Strong local community college and/or other post-secondary program	

STRATEGIES AND INITIATIVES—A FINAL WORD

This chapter presented 25 strategies and 18 initiatives designed to diversify local economies and improve overall quality of life. Arguably, the list of strategies represents the complete set of options available to communities. The list of Initiatives, on the other hand, is intended to be a partial list of options focused upon livability-enhancing measures for communities.

For a community to successfully implement these activities, and the strategies in particular, attention should be paid to the Key Success Factors. In additional to this logical assessment of relevant implementation factors, communities should also pay attention to the desires of the people of the community, as well as the human, financial and technical capacity available to implement such activities.

> **From Strategies and Initiatives to Action and Commitment**
>
> Next, Chapter Six will shift us from planning to action. The best strategic plan in the world is only a report sitting on the shelf if it is not acted upon. The principles for successful plan implementation are introduced.

CHAPTER SIX
Civic Action

CHAPTER SIX
Civic Action

Once a community has selected its community and economic development strategies and quality-of-life initiatives, it is time to act. The best strategic plan in the world is worthless if it is not acted upon. Plan your work, then work your plan.

Working the plan requires the coordinated energy of paid professionals and community volunteers all focused on the defined action steps of the plan. Similarly, our Two-Fruited Tree uses photosynthesis to convert light energy, normally from the sun, into chemical energy that can be used to fuel the tree's growth and production. Additionally, just as photosynthesis maintains oxygen levels and supplies the organic compounds and energy necessary for virtually all life on earth, the work of the people produces all of the fruit of jobs and better quality of life.

Just as the sun rises each day and the leaves of the tree form each spring, successful communities have people who regularly demonstrate commitment and action for the betterment of their city or town.

For communities, action steps follow the ready-aim-fire sequence. That is, for each of the strategies and initiatives, communities must be *ready* in terms of having an organized approach to implementation, *aimed* in terms of specific additional planning necessary for targeted implementation and *firing* in terms of actually taking the action necessary to execute the strategy and produce the fruit.

Organizing Action Steps (Ready!). Most of the strategies and initiatives have *organizing* action steps. These steps recognize that it takes one or more individuals to be responsible for the planning and execution of each strategy. Organizing can be as simple as identifying and designating an individual to be responsible for

Organizing Action Steps Examples
• Establishing a downtown development organization
• Creating a business retention outreach team
• Appointing an energy development task force
• Creating a committee to research funding sources
• Establishing a non-profit to support entrepreneurs
• Appointing a business incubator board of advisors
• Enhancing an existing agricultural extension office
• Spinning off a visitor and convention bureau from a chamber of commerce

the entirety of the planning and execution of the strategy, or it can be as broad as identifying several community organizations that will work together to plan and execute the strategy.

Planning Action Steps (Aim!).

The vast majority of strategies and initiatives will have *planning* steps. Once the individual(s) and/or organization(s) are in place to execute them, it will likely be necessary to put specific plans in place that define the future action necessary for implementation.

Planning Action Steps Examples
• Conducting a retail leakage study
• Researching local renewable energy resources
• Studying tourism expenditure patterns
• Conducting a target industry analysis
• Researching top community attribute preferences of retirees
• Identifying gaps in local health care services
• Researching composition of the local economy

The relative sophistication of a strategy- or initiative-specific planning step depends on its nature and complexity.

Execution Action Steps (Fire!).

Finally, every strategy and initiative selected will have execution action steps. These are the steps that are necessary to produce the intended outcomes (fruits) for each selection. Many performance measures that are associated with the community and economic development strategic

Execution Action Steps Examples
• Attending an industrial trade show
• Purchasing advertising in tourism publications
• Recruiting new physicians to the community
• Contacting a government agency to encourage their expansion in the community
• Building a performing arts center
• Building an industrial park
• Conducting a business expo
• Expanding a local community college

plan will most likely be measuring the success (or lack thereof) of execution action steps.

Assigning Action Steps

There are between four and 12 *essential* action steps for each strategy. That is, regardless of the community, a common set of organizing, planning and executing action steps exists per strategy (and initiative). Some examples are shown above in the three figures.

For a community that selects, for example, 10 strategies and five initiatives, this can mean the identification and assignment of approximately 100-150 action steps. Assigning action steps requires defining *who* is going to do *what* by *when*. That is, every step must come with very specific expectations of how the work is going to get done.

Assigning action steps can be overwhelming—if not done efficiently. It should the responsibility of a local steering committee—guided by a lead organization in the community—to ensure that the essential action steps are carefully assigned and executed.

The most efficient, and often most effective, method for assigning action steps is to immediately identify a lead organization for each strategy and initiative. The lead organization then becomes responsible for the assignment of the relevant action steps for their strategy(s)/initiative(s).

Short of assigning precisely who is going to do what by when, it is highly likely that nothing will be accomplished with the strategic plan. The community will stand still—or regress.

For more on how to assign action steps to a strategic plan, visit www.buildingcommunities.us/action-steps-planning-workshop.html.

From Civic Action to Civic Commitment

Next, Chapter Seven brings all of the concepts presented in this book into perspective. Megatrends slowly change. Civic condition evolves, albeit slowly. Civic capacity must always be tended to. Strategies and initiatives take time to implement. In short, community and economic development requires a long-term *commitment*.

CHAPTER SEVEN
Civic Commitment

CHAPTER SEVEN
Civic Commitment

The last step of the strategic planning and implementation process is to harvest the fruit. Community and economic development is all about diversifying the economy and creating the highest possible quality of life in cities, towns, counties and tribes across the county.

A diversified economy means that the current and emerging workforce, the community's next generation, and people looking to move to the community can find the jobs they desire. These jobs should not only meet their income needs, but they should also align with their skills, help fulfill their aspirations and provide them dignity. Ideally, people should do what they want to do to add value and make a living.

"It's the economy, stupid," has become one of the most popular catch phrases ever since James Carville posted it as one of three messages designed to help Bill Clinton unseat President George H.W. Bush in 1992. It worked. This remains one of the ultimate goals for virtually every community. Having a strong economy was consistently listed as the #1 issue in the Gallup Poll every time it was taken from February 2008 through October 2013. (Guess what replaced it? Dysfunctional Government!)

In addition to contributing to better economies, the second objective is improved livability for communities. Communities with high quality-of-life amenities offer their citizenry a safe, friendly and satisfying environment with neighborhoods that foster a healthy lifestyle. Creating and maintaining a sense of place contributes to quality of life. To achieve this, larger cities typically strive to minimize vehicle miles driven, and plan housing and transportation systems designed to minimize traffic congestion. Cities of all sizes strive to offer needed parks amenities and recreation programs, public safety services, and responsive government agencies and departments.

The Two-Fruited Tree represents these outcomes. Our mythical tree shows 16 business development strategies (for diversifying local economies, represented by pears) and nine community development strategies (for improved quality of life, represented by apples) that represent possible options for all communities. If the generation of fruit is the ultimate purpose for fruit trees, then the realization of benefits from implementing strategies and initiatives is the ultimate purpose of community and economic development activities.

The Human Analogy

The table below presents another dimension to consider. Just as the various components of a tree can represent elements of how a community functions, comparisons to the human body are instructive as well.

Chapter	Topic	Tree Analogy	Human Analogy
1	Two-Fruited Tree	Tree	
2	Economic Megatrends	Bedrock	
3	Civic Condition	Soil	Soul
4	Civic Capacity	Trunk	Body
5	Civic Strategies and Initiatives	Buds	Mind
6	Civic Action	Sunshine and Leaves	Heart
7	Civic Commitment	Fruit	

Like the human body, communities should understand and maintain the integrity of their heart, mind, body and soul. Analyzing and advancing a community reverses this familiar order: soul, then body, then mind, then heart.

For the whole community to successfully envision and enact its future, therefore, all four elements must be optimized. Indeed, the realization of a community's potential is only possible with a healthy civic condition (soul), strong civic capacity (body), wise deployment of strategies and initiatives (mind) and a concerted and enthusiastic pursuit of progress (heart).

The order of these human elements in their community context is important. Without a healthy civic condition, strong civic capacity is rendered virtually useless. Likewise, without sufficient civic capacity, the wise selection of strategies and initiatives is nearly irrelevant. Finally, selecting strategies and initiatives without taking action renders the entire effort fruitless.

Indeed, communities, like trees and humans, are living organisms with systems that must function in harmony.

The preface to this book illustrates the soul/body/mind/heart model in the context of the challenges to the United States of America as a nation.

Summarizing the First Six Chapters
Before offering principles for commitment to implementing effective community and economic development strategic plans, it is beneficial to summarize the lessons provided in the previous six chapters.

Chapter One: The Two-Fruited Tree. The illustration of the Two-Fruited Tree provides a visual to aid understanding the major concepts on which a successful community is based.

Chapter Two: Uncontrollable Economic Forces and Megatrends. Community leaders should not waste their time focused on uncontrollable factors and issues.

Chapter Three: Civic Condition. Community leaders should be mindful of their civic condition. To the extent possible, communities should encourage and strive to develop an *achievement* and *actualization* ethic.

Chapter Four: Civic Capacity. Business development and community development activities require sufficient human, financial and technical capacity for effective implementation.

Chapter Five: Civic Strategies and Initiatives. Strategies and initiatives should be selected based upon a thoughtful examination of a community's comparative advantages, desires and capacities.

Chapter Six: Civic Action. The implementation activities of a strategic plan should be rooted in the development of the plan itself, assigned to specific individuals and measured by their performance.

Principles for Effective Community and Economic Development Commitment
It is not enough simply just to understand these concepts. In order to advance communities, a process must be put in place to help communities mobilize efficiently and effectively. Any such process that ignores civic condition, short-changes civic capacity, does not fully consider all strategies and initiatives, and then fails to assign action steps, is designed for failure. In short, for communities to be successful there must be commitment to all four of these dimensions of civic life.

Considering Civic Condition. It is the overall civic condition (and related capacity) of the community that either contributes to—or compromises—the strategic planning and implementation process. This overall condition produces likely reactions and perceptions, which are summarized in the table and detailed in Chapter Three.

Reactions to the Planning and Implementation Process		
Civic Condition	Planning Phase	Implementation Phase
Apathy	Enjoyable, Positive	Disengaged, Disinterested
Argumentative	Regimented, Controlled	Selective, Forced
Action	Engaging, Productive	Collaborative, Effective
Alliance	Studious, Complete	Deliberate, Purposeful

Understanding the prevailing civic motivation can be very helpful to leaders and participants in the strategic planning process. Participants in the process are typically driven by a desire to contribute to their community. It is frequently difficult for individuals driven by a motivation of pure civic contribution to understand the broader dynamics and motivations of the community, especially if the motivations are different than the participants in the process.

The following table provides suggested actions community leaders and volunteers may wish to take in order to advance their strategic plan and community, while recognizing that motivations within the community differ.

The Four Stages of Civic Condition: Committing to Progress	
Stage	**Actions to Develop and Implement Strategic Plan**
Apathy Stage. Communities at the Apathy Stage are characterized by having little, if any, drive amongst their civic leaders (elected and non-elected). Perhaps the simplest test is: "How many people wake up on Saturday morning thinking about civic projects that are being advanced by the community?" While many communities have paid staff charged with advancing community development projects, are there individuals who are self-motivated to advance the project beyond any professional requirements? Apathy Stage communities are also characterized by a lack of vision and drive for community achievements. The community may be largely comprised of impressive individuals with other worthy values related to family and their religion but not those with a civic focus. These communities typically assume or decide that they cannot control their destiny, that state and federal government serves only as a regulator rather than a partner and that any attempts to change that philosophy will be doomed to failure.	The primary motivation for Apathy Stage leaders and volunteers is association. That is, such community members simply want to affiliate with one another in a social context. The challenge for achievement-oriented professionals and volunteers is to gain serious commitment from the community to advance local priorities. While people may show up to the planning process, especially if there is a good opportunity to socialize (and eat!), the key is to get people to dedicate themselves for the long-term. Recommended actions: • Select a small number of strategies and initiatives to include in the plan • Carefully select dates and times that Steering Committee members find most convenient for meetings • Provide snacks or rewards at the meetings • Celebrate small victories as the plan is being implemented • Be on the lookout for and reinforce new members who might want to make targeted commitments (specific projects or initiatives)
Argumentative Stage. Argumentative Stage communities move significantly forward on the *willingness continuum* but generally have not advanced on the *ability continuum*. Argumentative Stage communities are characterized by a group of civic leaders who do have goals and dreams for their community. These communities,	Argumentative Stage community leaders are typified by their behind-the-scenes power plays designed to carry out their personal agendas. The Argumentative Stage presents the greatest challenge to professionals and volunteers simply looking to improve their community. It is sometimes difficult for such altruistic volunteers to understand the gamesmanship that such power-grabbing people have, as it is so different from their own.

however, generally lack both the *professional capability* and the *unity* to carry these dreams forward.

Professional capability refers to a community's investment in an individual and/or organization that serves as an advocate. Although the individual need not be a paid professional, communities generally find this necessary in order create the stability needed for long-term advocacy.

Unity refers to the community's acceptance of the individual development projects being advanced. A lack of unity creates a dynamic in which the greatest obstacles to project advancement are created within the community itself.

Argumentative Stage communities frequently create a "lose-lose" dynamic.

Recommended actions:
- Co-opt one or more of the good ol' boys into the process by offering them power on one or more of the plan's priorities
- Withhold publicity on key projects or initiatives until such efforts are beyond being vulnerable to attack or subversion
- Invite power players to ceremonies and ribbon-cuttings; share the credit (even if undeserved)
- If possible, facilitate the desires of authority-seekers to serve on out-of-town boards and commissions

Action Stage. Action Stage communities are characterized by a track record of consistently identifying and advancing development projects. These communities have a high level of willingness and a high level of ability. They typically have a sense of overall direction whereby they can immediately identify whether or not proposed projects are consistent with that direction. Projects that are inconsistent are typically discarded. The rest are usually embraced and advanced.

Like Argumentative Stage communities, however, Action Stage communities are still faced with limited resources. While there are, at times, opportunities for collaboration among projects in Action Stage communities, typically the agenda becomes so large that competition for available technical and financial resources becomes a limiting factor. As such, Action Stage communities sometimes face a "win-lose" situation.

Action Stage communities generally have an army of professionals and (especially) volunteers dedicated to achieving all that is possible for their community.

The Action Stage setting is perfect for both planning and implementing the desired future of the community. People serving on Steering Committees will be right at home in their achievement-seeking environment.

Recommended actions:
- Invite a broad array of interests to the planning process
- Acknowledge and include existing projects and initiatives when developing the strategic plan
- Proactively promote the planning and implementation process to the community
- Ensure that implementation steps are broadly assigned in order to capture full implementation potential
- Use the planning process to broaden public awareness of the many strategies, initiatives and projects of the community

Alliance Stage. Alliance Stage communities take the ultimate step on the ability continuum. These communities are not only willing, but are also completely able to advance their development agenda. Like Action Stage communities, Alliance communities are skilled at envisioning, defining and advancing development projects. They have a record of success which reinforces a "we will succeed at this—it is only a matter of time" approach.

Alliance Stage communities make a paradigm shift from project orientation to community orientation. That is, it is simply not enough to succeed with advancing community development projects—it is necessary to examine how each of these projects serves larger community goals. Such communities strive for "win-win" solutions.

Alliance Stage communities are very rare. They have leaders who work to successfully elevate their Action Stage capabilities to actualize and sustain long-term progress.

While this stage should be the "ultimate level" of civic condition, there are some unique challenges to planning and implementation; as such communities can at times become preoccupied with process over results.

Recommended actions:
- Ensure that strategies and initiatives include action steps and assigned implementers
- Be wary of "analysis paralysis" (studying ideas to death)
- If certain strategies and initiatives seem to be falling victim to debate and study, consider advancing doable elements of such efforts

Assessing and Prescribing Civic Capacity. As described in Chapter Four, civic capacity relates to the human, financial and technical resources available to a community to plan and implement strategies and initiatives designed to strengthen local economies and bolster local quality of life.

While they are related and contribute to one another, business development (job-creating) capacity and community development (quality-of-life-producing) capacity are different, and should be considered separately. For example, the type of skills and resources a community needs to advance an Education Development strategy that might be focused upon the expansion of an existing community college are different from the types of skills and resources a community needs to recruit new industry. While both require networking and communications skills, the type of expertise related to financial matters, for example, differs.

Analyzing civic capacity should be very objective and specific. Broad statements such as "we need a more effective business development office" do not yield specific capacity-building activities. On the other hand, statements such as "by January 1, 2016, our business development advocacy needs an organization with a stable, long-term funding source designed to promote efficiency and effectiveness of staff and board performance" mobilize specific outcomes in terms of budget, board composition and staffing expectations.

While a baseline of civic capacity should be in place before the community invests heavily into staffing, training and travel, it should also be recognized that civic capacity grows (and sometimes shrinks) over time, and the best way to create long-term capacity is to embed such capacity in the actual activity of community and economic development implementation.

Recommended actions:

- Review Chapter Four, including all seven business development capacity elements and all seven community development capacity elements. Then read all of the capacity factors related to such elements

- Create an action plan designed to bolster the most important capacity factors

- Assign specific organizations, and people if possible, to each of the action steps

- Regularly meet to measure progress and performance

For the most holistic and specific assessment and prescription of civic capacity, visit www.buildingcommunities.us/community-organizer-assessment.html.

A more refined approach is to consider the capacity elements and factors that are most relevant to the specific strategies and initiatives included in the community's strategic plan. The level and type of capacity to implement a Leading-edge Development strategy, for example, is far different that the capacity needed to implement an Attracting Retirees strategy.

Advancing All Strategic Options. Perhaps the most common community and economic development mistake communities make is to only focus on a small subset of strategies and initiatives.

Time after time, communities think that the only relevant strategies are Business Recruitment and Business Retention and Expansion. In strategic plan after strategic plan, these are the only two strategies referenced. While it is true that the successful implementation of these strategies has a powerfully beneficial impact on a community, there are downsides to such a myopic approach:

- Business Recruitment is a long-shot and long-term activity. With successes few and far between, the community may go months and years without success

- Frequently, communities have groups and organizations that have other community development pursuits in mind (downtown or tourism development, for example). By excluding such groups, disputing or competing factions within the community begin to form

- Quality of life and overall livability factors contribute to business development success. By ignoring community development activities, the business development potential of the community is limited

The selection of the right number of strategies and initiatives is important. Chapter Five presents 25 Strategies and 18 Quality-of-life Initiatives, all of which are relevant to one or more communities. Selecting too few strategies limits the potential for the community. Selecting too many will place too great of a burden on civic capacity and cause the failure of many or most of the efforts.

Recommended actions:

- Fully consider all 25 Strategies, and select ones based upon the comparative advantages the community holds with respect to relevant Key Success Factors (as well as the desire of the people of the community)

- Answer the question: "What is affecting the quality of life in my community?" and then design, select and implement Quality-of-life Initiatives to preserve and enhance these livability priorities

- Include the general public in the strategic planning process

- If many strategies and initiatives are selected, consider phasing the implementation of some of them

Assigning Action Steps. Finally, as described in Chapter Six, assigning action steps is critical. Action does not happen by communities, action happens because specific people or groups within communities take it upon themselves to get the work done.

The best way to assign action steps is to do it collectively. That is, once the strategies and initiatives are selected, the group as a whole should identify "who is going to do what by when." Not only does this collective approach ensure efficiency (no two people duplicating effort), but accountability and momentum is built. When people see that others are willing to give of their time to their community, they will likely become more willing to step up.

Recommended actions:

- Begin the assignment of action steps in the strategic planning process itself

- Set a time limit (less than one month is recommended) to get the action steps assigned

- Create a work plan that includes each of the action steps for each of the strategies and initiatives

- Meet monthly to review progress on plan implementation

- Commit to plan implementation over the long haul (three to five years)

- Celebrate successes along the way

The Whole Tree, the Whole Body and the Whole Community

Western North Dakota is one of the fastest growing rural places in the world. The reason: it has a *super* Key Success Factor: *proximity to energy resources.* The volume of oil beneath its soil (and even down to its bedrock), combined with the speed that the resource is being extracted, is creating economic growth beyond the comprehension of anyone who has not visited the Bakken region (and many who have). Communities there will grow wildly even without the other three essential ingredients for successful communities: a healthy civic condition, strong community capacity and thought-out action steps.

And that is also the problem: they will grow *wildly.* Similarly, weeds can grow wildly in the poorest of soil (civic condition), and without any tending (civic capacity and civic action).

One can make an even harsher comparison to how cancer can grow wildly in the human body, and how a holistic approach to treatment is required to have the best chances for a successful outcome.

Fortunately, the western North Dakota region is taking proactive measures to grow purposefully and sustainably through local and regional strategic planning and implementation.

The point once again is that parallels can be drawn between the "intra-relationships" within the human, natural and built environments. Healthy communities must have a strong blend of condition/capacity/strategy/action similar to how trees must have supporting soil/trunks/leaves-sun/fruit and people have balanced souls/bodies/minds/hearts.

Closing Thoughts: Victory is Possible

The Four Stages of Civic Condition model, combined with a new approach to community and economic development strategic planning, offers the nation hope to reverse the alarming condition and trend of our politics and leadership. While some communities will still fail, more communities will succeed. There is something communities can do to successfully envision and enact their desired future.

Civic condition can be addressed if it is understood and positively acted upon.

Civic capacity can be enhanced by communities that are willing and able to make such investments.

Civic strategies and initiatives can be wisely selected and implemented if community leaders understand and focus upon Key Success Factors and consider the desires of their residents.

Civic action can be effective if essential action steps are understood and implemented.

Just as physicians can address the physical needs of people and horticulturists can address the physical needs of trees, community leaders and economic development professionals can and must wisely assess and prescribe the needs and possibilities for their community.

Community and economic development strategic planning, therefore, must ignore the uncontrollables, recognize and enhance the civic condition, build the civic capacity, prescribe the right civic strategies and initiatives, and then effectively act and implement.

America can turn the corner to a better tomorrow. Its communities hold the best prospect for such progress. Solutions are not simple, and this book offers a new approach to get there. One thing is certain: the alternatives to such progress are not acceptable.

Why Some Communities Succeed, Why Some Fail—and What to Do About It

EPILOGUE
Community Success and the Two-Fruited Tree

EPILOGUE
Community Success and the Two-Fruited Tree

Throughout this book, a connection is made between how communities function and the biology of a fruit tree. These excerpts are provided below.

		Why Some Communities Succeed, Why Some Fail— and What to Do About It
Ch.	Title	Tree Analogy Excerpts
1	The Two Fruited Tree	The figure at right, the *Two-Fruited Tree*, not only presents these sub-surface (uncontrollable) economic dynamics, but it represents a full spectrum of forces that shape the future of American (and worldwide) communities. This biomimicry not only shows the uncontrollable (subsurface) and controllable (above the surface) factors impacting communities, but it also shows the relationship between such factors. **Chapter One** Below the surface (of the earth) are the uncontrollable national and international economic forces that, while they do impact local economic conditions, they are well beyond the grasp of local decision makers. **Chapter Two** On the surface is the civic condition of the local community itself. This surface layer is so thin that it is rarely detected by the very people it impacts, and yet serves to predict the future success (or lack thereof) of community and economic development activities. **Chapter Three** Then there is the tree. The image of the two main trunks of the tree represents: 1) the business and economic development capacity (jobs), and 2) the community and quality of life capacity (livability) of the community. The relative strength of the trunk of the tree forms the foundation for producing the fruit (desired outcomes of community and economic development activities). **Chapter Four** The fruit on the tree, depicted by the two shapes (pears and apples), represents: 1) the business development (job creating) strategies, and 2) the community development (quality of life producing) strategies. **Chapter Five** Finally the leaves represent the energy of the community conducting the action needed to produce and harvest the fruit (jobs and quality of life). **Chapter Six**

2	**Uncontrollable Forces**	Throughout this book, a parallel is drawn between local community and economic development and the mythical Two-Fruited Tree. Here we begin with what holds up the tree—the earth. Specifically, deep beneath the surface of our communities is the earth's bedrock—a layer of solid un-weathered rock that lies beneath the loose surface deposits of soil. Unreachable. Impenetrable. Yet, a solid foundation. Similarly, national and international forces and megatrends are beyond the influence of local community leaders. While such large-scale economic dynamics either lift or depress local economic conditions, they are miles below the surface.
3	**Civic Condition**	This surface layer is, in effect, the soil that our Two-Fruited Tree draws its nutrients from. If the soil is inert or rocky, the tree will not produce. If the soil has the right texture, structure, consistency, chemical and biological characteristics, our tree will grow. Just as soil conditions form the foundation for a healthy and productive tree, the intent and quality of a community's civic discourse and interaction drives the potential future success (or lack thereof) of community and economic development efforts. If you were to look at a slice of the earth—all of the way through the planet—the soil at the edges of the slice would be so relatively thin as to be undetectable. At the same time, the surface of the planet is everywhere. The surface is under every city, every county and every nation. It is this thin, almost undetectable layer that perhaps best serves to answer the question: "why do some communities succeed and some communities fail?"
4	**Civic Capacity**	Civic Capacity is represented by the double trunk of the Two-Fruited Tree. The double trunk represents two distinct forms of capacity. Business development (job creating) capacity requires one set of elements while community development (quality of life producing) capacity requires another.
5	**Civic Strategies and Initiatives**	Getting back to our Two-Fruited Tree, the process of selecting strategies is represented by the phenomenon each spring of the forming of the buds on a tree. The buds are not yet the fruit, but they represent the potential benefits that the tree will yield in the months ahead. Just as the buds of the tree will yield fruit consistent with the physical characteristics of the tree, the community must examine its physical characteristics to determine which fruit (strategies and initiatives) it can produce.

6	Civic Action	Working the plan requires the coordinated energy of paid professionals and community volunteers all focused on the defined action steps of the plan. Similarly, our Two-Fruited Tree utilizes a process known as photosynthesis which converts light energy, normally from the sun, into chemical energy that can be used to fuel the tree's growth and production. Additionally, just as photosynthesis maintains oxygen levels and supplies all of the organic compounds and energy necessary for all life on earth, the work of the people produces all of the fruit of jobs and better quality of life. Just as the sun rises each day and the leaves of the tree form each spring, successful communities have people who regularly demonstrate commitment and action for the betterment of their city or town.	
7	Civic Commitment	The Two-Fruited Tree represents these outcomes. Our fictitious tree shows 16 business development strategies (for diversifying local economies, represented by pears) and nine community development strategies (for improved quality of life, represented by apples) that represent possible options for all communities. If the generation of fruit is the ultimate purpose for fruit trees, then the realization of benefits from implementing strategies and initiatives is the ultimate purpose of community and economic development activities.	

ABOUT THE AUTHOR

Brian Cole is a community and economic development professional with 27 years of experience in the field. Cole's driving passion is to transform the way communities envision and enact their future.

After establishing a community and economic development program in a rural community in the late 1980s, Cole was a regional development officer serving five rural counties.

After four years serving as a county commission chairman, Cole operated a community and economic development consulting firm before establishing Building Communities, Inc. in 2009.

Building Communities operationalizes the theories, tools and practices described in this book to offer a comprehensive, objective, expeditious, self-directed and action-oriented strategic planning process, which has been used by over 60 communities from coast to coast.

Cole holds a Master of Business Administration for Business, Government and Not-for-Profit Businesses from Willamette University and a Bachelor of Science in Business Administration from Oregon State University.

This is Cole's second book. He authored *Building Communities: 25 Strategies to Advance America* in 2009.

www.ingramcontent.com/pod-product-compliance
Lightning Source LLC
Chambersburg PA
CBHW081146280526
45787CB00008B/3246